Nonkilling Global Political Science

NONKILLING GLOBAL POLITICAL SCIENCE

GLENN D. PAIGE

First Published 2002. Second Edition 2007

Library of Congress Control Number: 00-193438

ISBN: Hardcover 978-0-7388-5744-2

Softcover 978-0-7388-5745-9

COVER IMAGE:

In the circle of the universe,

Creative transformational initiatives (blue),

drawing upon nonkilling human capabilities (white),

work to end human killing (red).

SYMBOL OF THE

CENTER FOR GLOBAL NONVIOLENCE

www.globalnonviolence.org

cgnv@hawaii.rr.com

This book was printed in the United States of America.

To order additional copies of this book, contact:

Xlibris Corporation

1-888-7-XLIBRIS

www.Xlibris.com

Orders@Xlibris.com

14994

Richard C. Snyder
1916–1997

H. Hubert Wilson
1909–1977

Political Scientists, Teachers, Friends

A science which hesitates to forget its founders is lost.

ALFRED NORTH WHITEHEAD

Contents

Preface

This book is offered for consideration and critical reflection primarily by political science scholars throughout the world from beginning students to professors emeriti. Neither age nor erudition seems to make much difference in the prevailing assumption that killing is an inescapable part of the human condition that must be accepted in political theory and practice. It is hoped that readers will join in questioning this assumption and will contribute further stepping stones of thought and action toward a nonkilling global future.

This may be the first book in the English language to contain the word "nonkilling" in its title. The term is not in customary use. It seeks to direct attention beyond "peace" and even "nonviolence" to focus sharply upon the taking of human life. The initial response of many may be that to focus upon nonkilling is too negative, too narrow, and neglects more important things. They may find company in Gandhi's admonition that to define *ahimsa* (nonviolence: noninjury in thought, word, and action) as nonkilling offers little improvement over violence.

Yet perhaps even Gandhi as reader, on reflection, might be persuaded that concentration upon liberation from killing as source and sustainer of other forms of violence could be a significant step forward in the political science of nonviolence. And from the politics of taking life to the politics of affirming it.

The thesis of this book is that a nonkilling global society is possible and that changes in the academic discipline of political science and its social role can help to bring it about. The assumption that killing is an inevitable attribute of human nature and social life that must be accepted in the study and practice of politics is questioned as follows. First, it is accepted that humans, biologically and by conditioning, are capable of both killing and nonkilling. Second, it is observed that despite their lethal capability most humans are not and have not been killers. Third, nonkilling capabilities already have been demonstrated in a wide range of social institutions that, if creatively combined and adapted, can serve as component contributions to realize nonkilling societies. Fourth, given present and expectable scientific advances in understanding of the causes of killing, the causes of nonkilling, and causes of transition between killing and nonkilling, both the psychobiological and social factors conducive to lethality are taken to be capable of nonkilling transformative intervention. Fifth, given the foregoing, the role of lethal human nature as the basis for acceptance of violence in political science and politics must at the very least become problematical as a foundation of the discipline. Sixth, in order to advance toward universally desired elimination of lethality from local and global life, political scientists who are presently not persuaded of human capacity for nonkilling social transformation are invited to join in taking up the possibility as a problem to be investigated hypothetically in terms of pure theory, combining inductive and deductive elements. Hypothetical analysis and role-playing by skeptics as well as by those who accept the possibility of nonkilling transformations can markedly assist disciplinary advance. Just as nuclear deterrence advocates and critics have been able to engage in theoretical and simulated exploration of local and global effects of limited or full-scale nuclear war, nonkilling and violence-accepting political scientists can join in constructively and critically exploring the preconditions, processes, and consequences of commitments to realize nonkilling conditions of global life.

Although this book is addressed primarily to those who study and practice political science, it is obvious that nonkilling societies cannot be realized without the discoveries and contributions of all scholarly disciplines and vocations. A magnificent example is Harvard sociologist Pitirim A. Sorokin's pioneering advance toward an applied science of altruistic love in *The Ways and Power of Love* (1954). Another is the unprecedented WHO *World Report on Violence and Health* (2002) which concludes that human violence is a "preventable disease." We need nonkilling natural and biological sciences, nonkilling social sciences, nonkilling humanities, nonkilling professions, and nonkilling people in every walk of life. Furthermore, in order to understand the full range of past and present human capabilities, we must share knowledge and experience beyond the bounds of local contexts and cultures. To be normatively sensitive, cognitively accurate, and practically relevant, nonkilling political science in conception and participation must be global.

Reader reflections and more than twenty translations being made of this book since first publication in 2002 foretell that global consideration of its nonkilling thesis will be forthcoming.

Acknowledgments

No acknowledgment can adequately express the depth and breadth of obligation to all whose contributions, past and present, known and unknown to them, have made this book possible. A glimpse can be seen here and in the bibliography. I am grateful to the people of Hawai'i whose labors supported this scholarly journey of discovery, to University of Hawai'i students from many lands who joined it to explore "Nonviolent Political Alternatives" in undergraduate courses and graduate seminars during 1978-1992, and to doctoral researchers on nonviolence who have gone on to careers of scholarly service such as Francine Blume, Chaiwat Satha-Anand, and Macapado A. Muslim.

In presenting this book I am especially aware of the influence of two great Princeton politics teachers, Richard C. Snyder and H. Hubert Wilson. To Snyder is owed respect for science, interdisciplinary outreach, the sense that the essence of politics resides in capacity to choose among alternatives, concern for education at all levels, and appreciation that values can serve as spotlights to illumine things that those without such values might not see. To Wilson, as later to Gandhi, is owed the example that a free and just society requires scholars and citizens prepared to speak for truths as they see them, even if it sometimes means to stand alone.

Like all scholars, I have benefited from many sources of inspiration and instruction within and beyond the academic community. Among spiritual leaders, I am especially indebted to Acharyas Tulsi and Mahapragya, Rabbi Philip J. Bentley, Rev. Sidney Hinkes, Daisaku Ikeda, Sr. Anna McAnany, Lama

Doboom Tulku, Fr. George Zabelka, and Abdurrahman Wahid. Among natural, biological and social scientists, to Ahn Chung-Si, Chung Yoon-Jae, James A. Dator, Johan Galtung, Piero Giorgi, Hong Sung-Chick, Lee Jae-Bong, Brian Martin, Ronald M. McCarthy, Bruce E. Morton, Kinhide Mushakoji, Eremey Parnov, Ilya Prigogine, L. Thomas Ramsey, Rhee Yong-Pil, Hiroharu Seki, William Smirnov, Leslie E. Sponsel, Gene Sharp, and Ralph Summy. Among humanities scholars, to A.L. Herman, Richard L. Johnson, Michael N. Nagler, Chaman Nahal, George Simson, Tatiana Yakushkina, and Michael True. Among librarians, Ruth Binz and Bruce D. Bonta. Among political and social leaders, James V. Albertini, M. Aram, A.T. Ariyaratne, Danilo Dolci, Gwynfor Evans, Hwang Jang-Yop, Petra K. Kelly, Jean Sadako King, Mairead Corrigan Maguire, Abdul Salam al-Majali, Ronald Mallone, Ursula Mallone, Andrés Pestrana, Eva Quistorp, Shi Gu, Ikram Rabbani Rana, Sulak Sivaraksa, and T.K.N. Unnithan. Among educators, Jose V. Abueva, N. Radhakrishnan, G. Ramachandran, Joaquín Urrea, and Riitta Wahlström. Among nonviolence trainers, Dharmananda, Charles L. Alphin, Sr., and Bernard LaFayette, Jr. Among physicians of body and spirit, Tiong H. Kam, Jean R. Leduc, Ramon Lopez-Reyes, Rhee Dongshik, Roh Jeung-Woo, and Wesley Wong. Among champions of innovation, Vijay K. Bhardwaj, Karen Cross, Larry R. Cross, Vance Engleman, S.L. Gandhi, Sarah Gilliatt, Lou Ann Ha'aheo Guanson, Manfred Henningsen, Theodore L. Herman, Sze Hian Leong, Anthony J. Marsella, Richard Morse, Romola Morse, Scott McVay, Hella McVay, Gedong Bagoes Oka, Burton M. Sapin, Stanley Schab, William P. Shaw, Joanne Tachibana, Voldemar Tomusk, John E. Trent and Alvaro Vargas.

To readers from varied perspectives who have generously commented upon the draft manuscript of this book I am profoundly grateful: Ahn Chung-Si, A.T. Ariyaratne, James MacGregor Burns, Chaiwat Satha-Anand, Vance Engleman, Johan Galtung, Luis Javier Botero, Amedeo Cottino, Elisabetta

Forni, Lou Ann Ha'aheo Guanson, Kai Hebert, Theodore L. Herman, Hong Sung-Chick, Edward A. Kolodziej, Ramon Lopez-Reyes, Caixia Lu, Mairead Corrigan Maguire, Brian Martin, Melissa Mashburn, John D. Montgomery, Bruce E. Morton, Muni Mahendra Kumar, Vincent K. Pollard, Ilya Prigogine, N. Radhakrishnan, Fred W. Riggs, James A. Robinson, Burton M. Sapin, Namrata Sharma, George Simson, J. David Singer, Chanzoo Song, Ralph Summy, Konstantin Tioussov, Voldemar Tomusk, Michael True, S.P. Udayakumar, T.K.N. Unnithan, Alvaro Vargas and Baoxu Zhao. Their comments have underscored the fertility of its thesis and obstacles to its realization. Responsibility for inadequacy in responding to their wisdom remains my own.

I am profoundly grateful to James A. Robinson, the first reader of the initial draft manuscript in February 1999, for his collegial offer in the spirit of Richard C. Snyder to contribute an introduction.

For typing the manuscript as she has done for every essay and book for more than twenty-five years, for administrative support, and for sharing journeys of nonviolent discovery in Bali, Bangkok, Beijing, Berlin, Brisbane, Hiroshima, London, Moscow, New Delhi, New York (UN), Paris, Provincetown, Pyongyang, Seoul, Tokyo, and Ulan Bator—in addition to her own career—I am ever grateful to Glenda Hatsuko Naito Paige.

Acknowledgment is made to the Columbia University Press for permission to reprint the excerpt from John W. Burgess, *Reminiscences of an American Scholar* (page 28), copyright © 1934 by Columbia University Press.

Introduction

THE POLICY SCIENCES OF NONKILLING

Caveat lector. The book you hold in hand, when read widely and taken seriously, will subvert certain globally prevailing values and the institutions that shape those values. Among such values, goals, preferences, demanded outcomes, events, and acts, as well as corresponding institutions, are those relating to the acquisition and use of power. "Power" designates the processes by which people participate in making decisions for themselves and others that bind them to comply, by coercion if necessary (Lasswell and Kaplan 1950: 75). Institutions associated with values of power include more than governments and their decision makers who wage war and apply severe sanctions including death to those who do not conform to public order. Interacting with power institutions are economies of organized entrepreneurs some of whom produce wealth from the inventions, manufactures, sales, and threats to use "arms"; universities among whose faculties some creative members conduct research and devise strategies of force and "coercive diplomacy"; associations of skilled athletes and artists that include those who specialize in violent games and entertainments; hospitals and clinics of venerated medical and health personnel who abort lives and assist in euthanasia; not so secret societies or "private armies" whose participants build and employ lethal weapons in defiance of or with tacit cooperation of public governments; families with members who perform or tolerate abuse among themselves, in some cultures even killing errant spouses, children, or in-laws; and certain religious organizations with faithful adherents who countenance killing deviants from approved doctrines, formulae, and miranda.

As every major sector of society implicates and is implicated by the power processes of its communities, so each supervises, regulates, employs, and corrects, with both positive and negative inducements, sometimes invoking killing, as in the security personnel who perform intimate functions in corporations, on college campuses, among entertainers, at hospitals and clinics, sometimes in family compounds and churches. The interactions between and among power institutions and other social institutions, insofar as they include killings or threats of killings, constitute problems of modern and postmodern societies, as noted by competent observers and expressed by alert participants.

Professor Glenn D. Paige systematically confronts these problems of individual, community, and global proportions, the problems of killing and threats of killing in human affairs. He defines the core of problems by demonstrating the empirical and logical discrepancies between, on the one hand, widely shared human claims, demands, preferences, and rights for minimum public and civic orders of dignity, and on another, the episodic contradictions and denial of those fundamental goals and objectives at virtually every level of social organization—small groups, localities, nations the world—and by varieties of institutions—governmental, economic, educational, skill, medical, social, familial, and religious.

The publication of this book now does not mean that the problems of killing are of recent origin or of sudden recognition. Nor does it mean that the book's appearance depends solely on the fortuitous application of the author's imagination and skills as scholar-scientist. Publication now rather than sooner means that despite the longstanding role, often acknowledged, of killing in human organizations and communities, men and women throughout the world have lacked an effective repertoire of problem solving approaches and tools to analyze, anticipate, and adopt alternative courses of policy that might diminish more effectively the probabilities of killing in favor of enhanced possibilities for nonkilling patterns of human interactions affecting all values in every arena.

Such a repertoire embraces the knowledge and skills accumulated among many academic, scientific, and scholarly persons despite or because of the killing around them and their institutions. Philosophers contribute to the formulation of problems, that is, to the postulation and clarification of the goal values and preferences frustrated in practice. Historians, demographers, economists, and others chronicle trends in the pathways of killing and nonkilling, and the rise and fall of human perspectives on all goals and preferences. Anthropologists, biologists, psychologists, and sociologists undertake to discover conditions underlying trends with a view to finding sites and occasions that might be conducive to interrupting gross deviant tendencies and promoting ever more frequent life affirming ones. Still others apply skill to forecasting or projecting paths of trends in the absence of interventions that might resist untoward trends and reinforce preferred ones. And among enlightened and experienced men and women of public affairs, the cadre of competent designers of applicable and feasible alternative courses of policy increase in number and sophistication. These men and women remain primarily in midelite rather than elite positions in which they might innovate in favor of nonkilling. Nevertheless, as specialists in enlightenment about human trends, conditions, and prospects, they present a formidable countervailing alternative to experts in violence who have made the last century among the bloodiest eras in the records of humankind while awaiting their rise to power with alternative predispositions and perspectives more favorably disposed toward human dignity. That the bloody twentieth century coincided with the emergence and institutionalization of the policy sciences of nonkilling constitutes a supreme, and welcome, irony.

Glenn Paige acquainted himself with the killing apparatus and capacities of his era by training for and fighting and killing in the Korean War. When he resumed his academic career, he began systematic preparation to be a teacher-scholar with an emphasis on relations among nations, particularly on the making and appraising of foreign policy decisions by key figures of governments (Snyder, Bruck, and Sapin 1962). Skilled in several languages as well as broadly educated in the social sciences, he has contributed importantly to a number of subfields of political science (e.g., Paige 1977). Midway in a half century of scholarship his analysis of personal goals brought him face to face with different perspectives on problems, goals, trends, conditions, and prospects of killing and alternative courses of action in education and public affairs to mitigate killing. His fundamental postulate became that prevailing conceptions of the state, notwithstanding occasional contrary voices, and scientific studies of the state are grounded in assumptions that emphasize killing over nonkilling. This book is the fruit of the second half of the author's long career and an attack on and an alternative to those assumptions, eventuating in the statement on behalf of nonkilling global political science now before the reader.

I have known the author for more than four decades of the period that we appreciate for its vast increases in enlightenment and deplore for its vast increases in the weight, scope, and domain of killing and threats to kill. Not friendship alone, or even respect, considerable as both are, motivate my joining in affirming the worth of this volume for those fellow world citizen-democrats in any arena of any community who identify with promoting nonkilling global behaviors. The motivation derives from many scientific and scholarly disciplines in humankind's shared interests in broad and peaceful as opposed to narrow and violent participation in shaping and sharing all values.

That this book comes from the work of a political scientist says something about its strength and weakness. "Political science" is the last of the social sciences to emphasize science as in modern conceptions of that word. As a "discipline," if it be worthy of such designation, its weakness is offset by the breadth of its boundaries. From this advantage came a new branch or orientation, "the policy sciences," emphasizing at once a multi-valued, multi-method, problem approach to social phenomena (Lasswell and McDougal 1992). Paige's work exhibits numerous equivalencies to, and contributes creatively to refinements in, the policy oriented social sciences of human dignity (Robinson 1999).

I write as one more familiar with institutions of enlightenment and power than any others, having lived, studied, taught, and administered in a variety of American colleges and universities for half a century, while specializing in the observation of power processes in various arenas at local, state, and national community levels in the United States and at varying levels in several other countries. That many of us overlook the presence of killing apparatus and personnel even in the cloister of college campuses is one of the lessons of my former administrative life. When noted, such killing and threats of killing are categorized and rationalized as the costs of doing business, and our colleges and universities indeed resemble business both from adaptations or emulations and also as pacesetters for business, commerce, and finance through our schools of administration, management, organization, and technologies.

The central role of force in political life is more apparent than in other social sectors. Not only is it virtually taken for granted in definitions of the state, but it underlies budgets of national governments for public order, internal security, foreign and defensive policies; appears in reliance of elected officials on sheriffs in political organizations and of force related industries for campaign contributions; and depends on the comfort and safety provided by community policemen near homes, schools, hospitals, and places of worship.

As the academic specialty concentrating on power institutions and their participants, political science might be expected to contribute to broad understanding of the roles and functions of force phenomena. It has, but a glance at the textbooks that introduce students to the subject matter of American politics, comparisons of national governments, and relations among nations would find force more a topic for inter-governmental transactions and violence as occasional cultural eccentricities than as core subjects. This restricted condition of modern political science makes welcome the focused conception proposed by Paige. Herein will be found the exercise of the important intellectual tasks relevant to clarifying goals, surveying trends, and understanding underlying factors which if unchecked will continue rather than alleviate problems of killing.

Here is the beginning of a reversal in the global policies that despite other benign trends contribute to but might counter killing. This is the foundation of efforts to encourage the further evolution of nonkilling alternatives. Such efforts supplement chance with positive actions that coincide with perspectives rooted in the emerging sciences of cultural evolution, sometimes called "memetic evolution," to be distinguished from similar processes of "genetic evolution." Theories of cultural evolution or co-evolution find increasing prominence in journals and books. Although these theories have yet to be congealed into a generally accepted framework, one of the earliest formulations is also among the most succinct and accessible. We may rely on it to suggest the emerging possibilities for steering further evolution of nonkilling ideas, institutions, and practices (Dawkins, 1976 and 1989).

Nonkilling as a "meme"—theme, symbol, idea, practice—survives or perishes like all other memes, and, so some theorists expect, like genes. To live or die depends on imitation or emulation. And the repetition or replication of a meme is enhanced by the longevity of the concept itself, which gives nonkilling an advantage in memetic development. The advantage resides in human memories and libraries of prayers, beliefs, songs, poems, and other expressions of pacific perspectives and operations. In addition to being preserved in cultural memories, nonkilling practices are reproduced easily, as in the number of nations that have disavowed armies, of communities that have abolished death penalties, of institutions of peace research, of services for dispute mediation and conflict resolution.

To hint at the fecundity of nonkilling practices is to indicate how easily these practices can be copied and have been copied. Moreover, precise copy fidelity is not necessary to keep alive ideas and institutions of nonkilling; indeed, variations from culture to culture, class to class, interest to interest, person to person, situation to situation, offer experiments in the effectiveness of alternative nonkilling policies.

The condition perhaps most related to successful and continuing replication of a memetic innovation is the complex of supportive or unsupportive sources into which it enters. A renewed emphasis in favor of nonkilling hardly could occur at a more fortuitous period, given changing conditions in several value sectors of world society. Consider that the twentieth century marked the arrival and consolidation of the first genuinely democratic states and their diffusion throughout the world in less than a hundred years (Karatnycky 2000). Even allowing for cases of regression or slow downs in the rate of expansion, prospects for continuing not to mention furthering democratization are bright. And evidence accumulates that rulers in democratic regimes are less likely to go to war with each other than those in undemocratic regimes (Oneal and Russett 1999; for qualification, see Gowa 1999). Likewise, democratic rulers more probably will pursue policies that avoid famines than nondemocratic governors (Sen 1999: 16, 51-3, 155-7, 179-82).

On the heels of the democratic era came post modern concern for broad participation in the shaping and sharing of all values, not just power or wealth. The world wide devotion to respect, self respect and respect for others, supports nonkilling innovations. Similar memes take form even in the killing institutions, as police learn to handle crises of riots and protests more skillfully as well as more peacefully, as professional military personnel adopt globally professional norms reaching beyond the reach of force. And in other sectors of society also, alternatives to abuse and killing appear, as in Favor Houses, curricula in nonviolence, and in broadened conceptions of conscientious objection status.

The promotion of evolutionary biases in favor of nonkilling depends ultimately on more than will and dedication, more than the goodwill of public opinion, but also on secure bases of knowledge from which alternative courses of action may be designed, implemented, and appraised. Hence, the immense importance of a political science of nonkilling.

Therefore, respected reader, you have presented to you a work of science and policy. You are entitled, indeed urged, to suspend judgment until you have encountered the case for a nonkilling global political science. If unconvinced, you can take comfort amid a silent but continuing effective plurality who explicitly or implicitly accepts killing and threats of killing as constitutional. If persuaded, you will find a niche in the complex panoply of opportunities suggested in this book to join in mobilizing the enlightenment and energy of men and women of similar perspectives among every culture, class, interest, and personality type in situations of whatever level of crisis or stress in promoting and favoring strategies of persuasion over those of coercion in every arena affecting all the values of a potentially global commonwealth of human dignity.

James A. Robinson

Pensacola, Christmas Day, 1999
Beijing, New Year's Day, 2000

REFERENCES

DAWKINS, RICHARD. 1989. *The Selfish Gene.* Oxford: Oxford University Press.

GOWA, JOANNE. 1999. *Ballots and Bullets: The Elusive Democratic Peace.* Princeton: Princeton University Press.

KARATNYCKY, ADRIAN. 2000. The 1999 Freedom House survey: a century of progress. *Journal of Democracy,* 11 (1): 187–200.

LASSWELL, HAROLD D. and KAPLAN, ABRAHAM. 1950. *Power and Society: A Framework for Political Inquiry.* New Haven, Conn.: Yale Univesity Press.

LASSWELL, HAROLD D. and McDOUGAL, MYRES S. 1992. *Jurisprudence for a Free Society: Studies in Law, Science and Policy.* New Haven, Conn.: New Haven Press and Dordrecht: Martinus Nijhoff Publishers. 2 vols.

ONEAL, JOHN R. and RUSSETT, BRUCE. 1999. The Kantian peace: the pacific benefits of democracy, interdependence, and international organizations. *World Politics,* 52 (1): 1–37.

PAIGE, GLENN D. 1977. *The Scientific Study of Political Leadership.* New York: The Free Press.

ROBINSON, JAMES A. 1999. Landmark among decision-making and policy analyses and template for integrating alternative frames of reference: Glenn D. Paige, *The Korean Decision. Policy Sciences* 32: 301–14.

SEN, AMARTYA. 1999. *Development as Freedom.* New York: Knopf.

SNYDER, RICHARD C.; BRUCK, HENRY W.; and SAPIN, BURTON, eds. 1962. *Foreign Policy Decision Making: An Approach to the Study of International Politics.* New York: The Free Press of Glencoe, Macmillan.

Chapter 1

IS A NONKILLING SOCIETY POSSIBLE?

> Philosophy begins when someone asks a general question, and so does science.
>
> Bertrand Russell

> The questions that a country puts are a measure of that country's political development. Often the failure of that country is due to the fact that it has not put the right question to itself.
>
> Jawaharlal Nehru

Is a nonkilling society possible? If not, why not? If yes, why?

But what is meant by a "nonkilling society"? It is a human community, smallest to largest, local to global, characterized by no killing of humans and no threats to kill; no weapons designed to kill humans and no justifications for using them; and no conditions of society dependent upon threat or use of killing force for maintenance or change.

There is neither killing of humans nor threat to kill. This may extend to animals and other forms of life, but nonkilling of humans is a minimum characteristic. There are no threats to kill; the nonkilling condition is not produced by terror.

There are no weapons for killing (outside museums recording the history of human bloodshed) and no legitimizations for taking life. Of course, no weapons are needed to kill—fists or feet suffice—but there is intent neither to employ this capability nor technologically to extend it. Religions do not sanctify lethality; there are no commandments to kill. Governments do not legitimize it; patriotism does not require it; revolutionaries do not prescribe it. Intellectuals do not apologize for it; artists do not celebrate it; folk wisdom does not perpetuate it; common sense does not commend it. In computer terms of this age, society provides neither the "hardware" nor the "software" for killing.

The structure of society does not depend upon lethality. There are no social relationships that require actual or threatened killing to sustain or change them. No relationships of dominance or exclusion—boundaries, forms of government, property, gender, race, ethnicity, class, or systems of spiritual or secular belief—require killing to support or challenge them. This does not assume that such a society is unbounded, undifferentiated, or conflict-free, but only that its structure and processes do not derive from or depend upon killing. There are no vocations, legitimate or illegitimate, whose purpose is to kill.

Thus life in a nonkilling society is characterized by no killing of humans and no threats to kill, neither technologies nor justifications for killing, and no social conditions that depend upon threat or use of lethal force.

Is a nonkilling society possible?

* * * * *

Our answers will be conditioned by personal experience, professional training, culture, and context—all factors that political scientists employ to explain the behavior of others—influences from which we ourselves are not immune.

* * * * *

It's absolutely unthinkable!

Such was the virtually unanimous response of a group of twenty American political scientists when asked a somewhat similar question during a summer seminar sponsored by the National Endowment for the Humanities in 1979 to review classics of Western political thought for use in college teaching. The question then asked was, "Are nonviolent politics and nonviolent political science possible?" Four major fields of American political science were represented equally in the seminar: political theory, American government, comparative politics, and international relations. All scholars save one were males.

Three quick arguments decisively settled the question in a brief seminar-end discussion. First, humans by nature are killers; they are dangerous social animals always liable to kill. Second, scarce resources will always cause competition, conflict, and killing. Third, the ever-present possibility of rape requires male readiness to kill to defend related females. (The comparable American woman's argument went unvoiced: "If anyone threatens the life of my child, I'll kill him." Also unasked was the customary counter-question assumed sufficient to silence further thought about the possibility of nonkilling politics: "How are you going to stop Hitler and the Holocaust by nonviolence?") The primal arguments of human nature, economic scarcity, and sexual assault served sufficient to make unthinkable the practice and science of nonkilling politics.

Reference to the freshly reviewed classics of Western political thought also was unnecessary. Their mastery, like that of the punitive Legalist tradition in China and the crafty Kautilyan tradition in India, predisposes to the same conclusion. Explicitly or implicitly readiness to kill is deemed essential for the creation and defense of the good society.

In Plato's (427-347 B.C.E.) ideal *Republic,* philosopher rulers (Guardians) recruited from the warrior class (Auxiliaries) rule over Producers and Slaves by coercion and persuasion. Furthermore, as Leon Harold Craig notes, "An unprejudiced observer can scarcely avoid concluding that (in Plato's *Republic*) war must be regarded as the fundamental fact of political life, indeed of all life, and that every decision of consequence must be made with that fact in mind." (Craig 1994: 17; cf. Sagan 1979). In Aristotle's (384-322 B.C.E.) *Politics,* in preferred polities—whether ruled by one, few, or many—property owners bear arms, and armies are essential to keep slaves in submission and to prevent enslavement by enemies. Neither Plato nor Aristotle questions the permanent presence of military lethality.

The much admired Machiavelli (1469-1527) in *The Prince* contributes explicit justification for rulers to kill to maintain their positions of power and to advance the *virtu,* fame, and honor of their states. It is better to rule by craftiness of a "fox," but when necessary rulers should not shrink from the bold lethality of a "lion." He prescribes citizen militias to strengthen the power of the republican state.

Thomas Hobbes (1588-1679) in *Leviathan* provides further justification for killing by governments to secure social order and victory in war. Since humans are killers, unorganized life in a state of nature results in murderous chaos. But since humans are also survival-seekers, they must consent to obey a central authority empowered to kill for their security, while reserving to themselves the inalienable right to kill in self-defense. Hobbes stops short of justifying armed rebellion.

This is done by John Locke (1632-1704) in *Two Treatises of Government.* Locke agrees with Plato, Aristotle, Machiavelli, and Hobbes that political rule necessitates readiness to kill. But he goes further to justify revolutionary lethality. When the sovereign authority becomes tyrannical and violates inherent rights to property, liberty, and life—oppressed citizens have the right and duty to destroy it. Just as a murderer may be killed in a state of nature, citizens in civil society may destroy a despotic ruler.

The Hobbes-Locke double justification for ruler-ruled lethality is extended into economic class warfare by Karl Marx

(1818-1883) and Friedrich Engels (1820-1895) in *The Communist Manifesto.* Propertied classes can be expected to defend and extend their interests by lethal force. But when material and social relations reach a critical stage, exploited classes can be expected to rise in violent rebellion to change the economic and political structure of society. In a few special cases of modern electoral democracy peaceful change might be possible. Sometime in the future when economic exploitation ends, the class-based lethal state will disappear. But in the period of transition economic factors will predispose to killing.

Writing between Locke and Marx, echoing Hobbes, Jean-Jacques Rousseau (1712-1778) in *The Social Contract* presents the theory of a "social contract" as the basis for political organization of the state. Citizens collectively constitute both the sovereign authority and subjects of the state. They commit themselves to obey a ruling authority that makes and administers laws derived from the "general will." Under the contract the state claims the right of war and conquest, traitors can be executed, and criminals can be killed. The ruling body can order citizens to sacrifice their lives for the state:

> Quand le prince lui à dit: Il est expedient à l'État que tu mueres, il doit mourir; puisque . . . sa vie n'est plus seulement un bienfait de la nature, mais un don conditionnel de l'État.
>
> *Du contrat social* Livre II, chapitre v.

> When the ruling authority has said to a citizen: It is expedient for the State that you should die, he must die; since . . . his life is no longer only a benefaction from nature, but is a conditional gift from the State.
>
> *The Social Contract* Book II, chapter v.

Ultimately Rousseau's democratic social contract is a compact with lethality.

In the twentieth century, Max Weber (1864-1920), influential German political economist and sociological theorist, in "Politics as a Vocation," originally a University of Munich speech in 1918, categorically dismisses the idea that politics can be a nonkilling profession. For Weber, "the decisive means for politics is violence." Historically all dominant political institutions have arisen from violent struggles for power. Consequently Weber defines the modern state as "a human community that (successfully) claims *the monopoly of the legitimate use of physical force within a given territory* (emphasis in original)." Therefore, "he who seeks the salvation of the soul, of his own and that of others, should not seek it along the avenue of politics, for the quite different tasks of politics *can only be solved by violence* (emphasis added)" (Weber 1958: 121, 78, 126).

Thus it is understandable that professors proficient in the Weberian tradition and its philosophical predecessors should consider nonkilling politics and nonkilling political science to be "unthinkable." The underlying professional orientation was succinctly expressed in the response of a senior American political scientist in the 1950s to a young scholar who asked him to share his definition of "politics," the subject of his lifelong study. He puffed on his pipe and replied, "I study the death-dealing power of the state."

Furthermore, echoes of the lethal philosophical tradition, blessed by violence-accepting religion, resonate throughout United States political history and culture, strongly reinforcing citizen-scholar beliefs that a nonkilling society is impossible. They are heard in the musket fire at Lexington that sparked the American Revolution, in the ringing Lockean justifications for revolt proclaimed by the Declaration of Independence, and in New Hampshire's defiant cry "Live Free or Die!" They are heard in the "Battle Hymn of the Republic," inspiring Union victory over Confederate rebellion, as well as in "Dixie's" lingering defiant refrain, and in the "Marine Hymn," celebrating distant battles on land and sea. They resound in the twenty-one gun salute that honors the inauguration of the President as Commander-in-Chief, a reminder of the nation's violent past and present military power. Throughout a lifetime they are repeated in ceremonial combination of flag, anthem, and armed escort, evoking emotions of sacrifice and slaughter, sanctified by the presidential benediction "God bless America" (Twain 1970).[1]

Killing contributed to the origins, territorial expansion, national integration, and global power projection of the United States of America. The dead and wounded, domestic and foreign, military and civilian, remain unsummed and are perhaps incalculable, but the reality of American state lethality is undeniable. Political scientists in other countries are called upon to reflect upon contributions of more or less killing to their own political identities.

The new nation began in armed republican revolt against monarchical colonial rule, while keeping slaves in subjugation. Under the flag of liberty it expanded its continental domain by bloody conquest of indigenous peoples, by force against neighbors to the north and south, and by cession or purchase from proprietors preferring commerce to combat. The state coerced national integration by Civil War, killing 74,542 Confederate soldiers and sacrificing 140,414 Union dead.

Extending itself overseas the American state gained control over Hawai'i (1898); Puerto Rico, Guam, and the Philippines (1898); eastern Samoa (1899); and Pacific island territories (1945). In the Philippines it suppressed anti-colonial rebellion (1898-1902) and slaughtered Muslim Moros who resisted assimilation (1901-13). By naval threat it opened isolationist Japan to foreign trade (1853-54).

By wars and interventions the emerging nation projected and defended its interests. Among wars it fought against Britain (1812-14), Mexico (1846-48), Spain (1898), Germany, Austria-Hungary, Turkey and Bulgaria (1916-18), Japan, Germany, and Italy (1941-45), North Korea and China (1950-53),

North Vietnam (1961-75), Afghanistan (2001-) and Iraq (1991, 2003-). Among armed interventions were those in Peking (1900), Panama (1903), Russia (1918-19), Nicaragua (1912-25), Haiti (1915-34), Lebanon (1958), the Dominican Republic (1965-66), and Somalia (1992). By invasions the United States overthrew governments in Grenada (1983) and Panama (1989), and by threat of invasion in Haiti (1992). By invasions or attacks it sought to interdict in Cambodia (1970) and Laos (1971), to retaliate in Libya (1986), Afghanistan (1998), and Sudan (1998); and to demonstrate will to advance strategic interests in Iraq (1993), Bosnia (1995), and Yugoslavia (1999).

During a half century of post-WWII worldwide struggle against anti-capitalist states, revolutionaries, and other enemies, the United States extended its lethal capabilities to encompass the globe. From less than one thousand men in the Revolutionary era the nation's regular armed forces by the 1990s had grown to 1.5 million men and women, backed by 23,000 Pentagon planners, an innovative scientific elite, and the world's most advanced weapons industry—all made possible by annual commitments of at least a quarter trillion taxpayer dollars approved by the Congress and the President. It was conservatively calculated that the nation's nuclear weapons program alone during 1940-96 had cost the nation 5.821 trillion dollars (Schwartz 1998). The United States had more overseas bases, more forces deployed abroad, more military alliances, and was training and arming more foreign forces (killers of its enemies, sometimes of its friends, and even of its own people) than any other country. Concurrently it had become the leading supplier of weapons in the world's competitive, lucrative, arms market. Technologically the United States had become capable of projecting killing force throughout the land, sea, and air space of the planet by means of the most destructive weapons yet devised by the lethal ingenuity of humankind.

By the 1990s the battle-born United States had proceeded from declaration of independence in 1776 to proclaim itself as "the world's only military superpower and the world's leading economy" (President William J. Clinton, State of the Union Address, February 19, 1993). In the words of the chairman of the Joint Chiefs of Staff, Army General John Shalikashvili, the United States had become a "global nation" with "global interests." Celebrating in 1995 the fiftieth anniversary of the atomic-bomb victory over Japan, the President in Hawai'i pledged to the assembled troops of all services, "You will always be the best trained, best equipped fighting force in the world." He declared, "We must remain the strongest nation on earth so as to defeat the forces of darkness in our era." This determination was reflected in a 1996 explanation of Air Force strategic planning by Chief-of-Staff General Ronald Fogelman, "Our goal is to find, fix, track, and target everything that moves on the face of the earth." He further revealed, "We can do it now, but not in real time" (not as it happens). (Speech at the Heritage Foundation, Washington, D.C., December 13, 1996).

As the twentieth century neared its end, American leaders were wont to claim it as "The American Century" and to express determination to make the first century of the third millennium "The Second American Century." Amidst such a triumphal tradition of the virtues of violence, a nonkilling United States of America is easily unthinkable. Killing and threats to kill created national independence, abolished slavery, defeated nazism and fascism, ended the Holocaust, saved lives in atom-bombed Japan, prevented global communist expansion, caused the collapse of the Soviet empire, and now secures the claim to be the leading force for diffusion of democratic freedom and capitalist economics throughout the twenty-first century world.

But for Americans who study political science, from senior professors to introductory students, neither philosophy nor national political tradition is needed for conviction that a nonkilling society is impossible. Killing in everyday life confirms it.

More than fifteen thousand Americans are murdered by other Americans each year (15,533 in 1999; 5.7 per 100,000 people, up from 1.2 in 1900). Reported murders do not include "justifiable homicides" by police or private citizens (294 and 188 in 1999). Total homicides since WWII (estimated to be at least 750,000) exceed battle deaths in all the nation's major wars (650,053). To homicides can be added "aggravated assaults" (916,383 in 1999; 336.1 per 100,000), attacks with weapons capable of causing death or grave injury (Federal Bureau of Investigation 2000: 13, 23, 32). Suicides contribute even more than homicide to life-taking in American civil society (31,284 in 1995; 11.9 per 100,000). Attempted suicides are twenty-five times greater. Annual abortions are estimated to be more than 1,000,000.

Americans kill by beating, beheading, bombing, and burning; drowning, hanging, pushing, and poisoning; stabbing, suffocating, strangling, and mostly by shooting (64.5% in 1999). Killings are premeditated, spontaneous, professional, and accidental. They accompany spouse abuse, child abuse, elder abuse, arguments, drunken brawling, drug dealings, gang fights, gambling, jealousy, kidnapping, prostitution, rape, robbery, cover-up, and "divine" or "satanic" commandments. No place is truly safe: homes, schools, streets, highways, places of work and worship, prisons, parks, towns, cities, wilderness, and the nation's Capitol. Victims are killed singly, serially, collectively and randomly; mostly male (76% in 1999). But among spouses killed during 1976-85 wives (9,480) outnumbered husbands (7,115) (Mercy and Saltzman 1989). Killers are individuals, couples, gangs, sects, syndicates, terrorists, and when engaged in law enforcement servants of the state. Known killers are predominantly male (9,140 compared to 1,046 females in 1999), and are becoming younger. In 1980 it was estimated that "for an American, the lifetime chance of becoming a homicide victim is about one in 240 for whites and one in 47 for blacks and other minorities" (Rosenberg and Mercy 1986: 376). As Senate majority leader Republican Trent Lott observed on national television in response to President Clinton's State of the Union Address on January 27, 1998: "Violent crime is turning our country from the land of the free to the land of the fearful."

The news media testify daily to American lethality. A daughter chops off the head of her mother, drives by a police station, and throws it out on the sidewalk. A mother drowns two sons; two sons murder their parents. A serial killer preys on prostitutes; a homosexual seduces, dismembers, refrigerates, and cannibalizes young victims. A sniper kills fifteen people at a university. Two boys with rifles at a rural middle school kill four girl classmates and a teacher, wounding another teacher and nine more schoolmates. Two heavily armed boys at Columbine High School in Littleton, Colorado kill thirteen classmates, wound 28, and commit suicide. During 1996-99, school students, aged 11 to 18, kill 27 fellow students, two teachers, three parents, and wound 65 others. A man with an automatic weapon slaughters urban school children on their playground. A Vietnam War veteran machine-guns customers at a fast-food family restaurant, killing 20, wounding 13. Still another clad in military combat fatigues massacres worshippers in a church, yelling "I've killed a thousand before and I'll kill a thousand more!"

Arrayed against fearful Hobbesian predations by fellow citizens and in Lockean distrust of the Weberian state, stands an armed people in possession of nearly two hundred million guns—at least 70 million rifles, 65 million handguns, 49 million shotguns, and 8 million other long guns (Cook and Ludwig 1997). The gun trade—manufacture, sales, import, and export—is big business with tens of thousands of dealers, legal and illegal. Firearms, owned by 44 million adults, are estimated to be present in at least one-third of American households. Most children know how to find them even if parents think they do not. The nation's first lady, Hillary Clinton, based upon estimates by the Children's Defense Fund, reports that 135 thousand children take guns and other weapons to school each day (Speech in Nashua, New Hampshire, February 22, 1996). Citizen gun possession is claimed for self-defense, hunting, recreation, and resistance to government tyranny as an inalienable right guaranteed by the 1791 Second Amendment to the United States Constitution: "A well-regulated militia, being necessary to the security of a free State, the right of the people to keep and bear Arms shall not be infringed."

Arrayed against the dangers of domestic lethality are the armed police of the American state. These include federal agents of law enforcement plus state and local police (641,208 officers in 1999; 250 per 100,000 people). Forty-two are killed in 1999 (Federal Bureau of Investigation 2000: 91). They are reinforced when needed by state units of the National Guard and by the federal Armed Forces of the United States. Prison guards stand watch over more than 1.8 million prisoners convicted of various crimes, including 3,527 awaiting execution in 1999 (Bureau of Justice 2000b; 2000a). The death penalty is in force for federal crimes and in thirty-eight of fifty states. Executions during 1977-99 totaled 598. As the twentieth century ends, amidst fears of rising crime and seemingly intractable violence, there are anxious cries to expand or reimpose the death penalty, to place more policemen on the streets, to impose longer prison sentences, and to build more prisons.

Violence in America is socially learned and culturally reinforced. Formally and informally, legally and illegally, people are taught how to kill. Over twenty-four million military veterans are graduates of professional training for lethality (24,800,000 in 1999). About one in four adult males are veterans. Many junior high schools, high schools, colleges, and universities provide preparatory military training. Businesses teach how to kill in self-defense. Private militias train for combat; street gangs socialize for killing; prisons serve as colleges of predation. Magazines for mercenaries teach techniques of combat, sell weapons, and advertise killers for hire. Video and computer "games" engage young "players" in simulated killing from street fighting to land, air, sea, and space combat, employing a wide range of lethal technologies. "Virtual reality" businesses sell "adrenaline-pumping," kill-or-be-killed recreational experiences. For a time a fad on college campuses is to play "assassination" of fellow students. Actual and simulated killing seem natural extensions of childhood play with toy weapons.

Vicarious learning for lethality and desensitization of the value of human life are provided by the mass media of communication. Teachers are creators of cartoons, films, television and radio programs, songs, books, magazines, and commercial advertisements. From childhood through adulthood thousands of violent images are imprinted upon the mind, demonstrating dramatic ways in which people, property, animals, and nature can be destroyed by heroes and villains. Increasingly images of bloodshed and brutality are combined in rapid alternation with images of sexuality, especially in preview advertisements for violent motion pictures, verging upon subliminal seduction for lethality.

No people in history have had so many lethal images imprinted upon their brains. Since a proven military technique for overcoming reluctance to kill in training commandos and assassins is to force them to view films of gruesome atrocities — head in vise with eyes propped open (Watson 1978: 248-51)— it is as if the whole nation is being desensitized from empathic respect for life to unemotional acceptance of killing. Judges report that juvenile killers increasingly evidence no respect for human life. But however harmful to civil society, violent media socialization is useful for a state in need of professional patriotic killers. This is epitomized by a million dollar recruitment advertisement shown during a televised Super Bowl American football game. Millions of viewers see a sword-wielding medieval knight from a video combat "game" metamorphose into a modern saber-saluting United States Marine.

Language reflects and reinforces lethality, contributing a sense of naturalness and inescapability. The American economy is based upon free enterprise capitalism. Americans speak of "making a killing on the stock market"; there is a Wall Street saying, "You buy when there's blood in the streets"; and businesses compete in "price wars." American politics are based upon free electoral democracy. Campaign workers are called "troops" or "foot soldiers"; bills are "killed" in legislatures; and the nation "wages war" on poverty, crime, drugs, and other problems. The national sport is baseball. When displeased, disgruntled fans traditionally yell "Kill the umpire!" Sports commentators refer to tough football teams as "killers"; players are called "weapons"; passes are called "long bombs; and losing teams are said to "lack the killer instinct." Taking pride in religious freedom, while worshipping the Prince of Peace, Americans sing "Onward Christian soldiers" and reflecting the spirit of the Christian Crusades and Reformation chorally climb "Jacob's ladder" as "soldiers of the Cross." As life passes, at idle moments they speak of "killing time."

While becoming increasingly conscious of the harmful effects of racist and sexist language, Americans continue to speak the language of lethality with unconcern. The linguistic "armory" of American English provides terms that evoke all the weapons known to history, ways of using them, and their effects. Betrayal is "a stab in the back"; budgets are "axed"; and attempt is "to take a shot at it"; ideas are "torpedoed"; opposition is termed "flak"; and consequences of actions are called "fall-out." Lawyers are "hired guns." A beautiful movie star is termed a "blonde bombshell."

On the other hand, euphemisms customarily cloak real killing. "Little Boy" the world's first atomic bomb is dropped on Hiroshima from a B-29 bomber named for the pilot's mother "Enola Gay." Next, plutonium bomb "Fat Man" is dropped by "Bock's Car" on Nagasaki. Intercontinental nuclear missiles capable of mass murder of urban populations are called "Peacemakers." Reversing the language of warfare applied to sports, military exercises to prepare for killing are called "games."

Killing of civilians or of our own troops in combat is called "collateral damage." As expressed by former President Ronald Reagan, "America is the least warlike, most peaceful nation in modern history" (PBS 1993).

Periodically elements of lethality in America combine in collective violence among citizens themselves and between them and agents of the state. In 1992, 52 people were killed, 2,000 were injured, and 8,000 were arrested in south central Los Angeles amidst shooting, looting, and arson in response to judicial exoneration of police brutality against a black citizen. Within two months some 70,000 guns were sold to fearful citizens in surrounding areas. The bloodshed is reminiscent of similar killings in Watts (34 in 1965), Newark (26 in 1967) and Detroit (46 in 1967) as well as of loss of life in slave uprisings of the eighteenth and nineteenth centuries. To restore order in Detroit in 1967 it took 4,700 Army paratroopers, 1,600 National Guardsmen, and 360 Michigan State troopers (Locke 1969).

The consequences of combining the Hobbesian-Weberian state with the Lockean Second Amendment legacy are exemplified by killings in Waco, Texas, in 1993 and in Oklahoma City, Oklahoma in 1995. In Waco, armed agents of the state seek to enforce laws against an armed religious sect: four federal officers are killed, a dozen are wounded, and 89 members of the sect, including women and children, die in a fiery conflagration. On the second anniversary of this tragedy, in apparent revenge, an antagonist of the state detonates a truck bomb to demolish the federal office building in Oklahoma City, killing 168, including women and children.

Looking beyond their borders Americans see ample evidence to confirm conviction that a nonkilling society is impossible. The twentieth century, mankind's most murderous era, demonstrates the horror of human capacity to kill on a massive scale. Research by Rudolph J. Rummel permits placing the bloodshed in historical and global perspective. Distinguishing between "democide" (state killing of its own people by genocide, execution, mass murder, and manmade famine), and battle deaths in "war" (world, local, civil, revolutionary, and guerrilla), Rummel calculates "conservatively" the magnitude of killing in recorded history as in Table 1.

TABLE 1

DEATHS BY DEMOCIDE AND WAR TO 1987

	PRE-1900	1900-1987	TOTAL
DEMOCIDE	133,147,000	169,198,000	302,345,000
WAR	40,457,000	34,021,000	74,478,000
TOTAL	173,604,000	203,219,000	376,823,000

Source: Rummel 1994: Table 1.6; 66-71.

Thus perhaps as many as four hundred million people might be counted victims of historical political killing, not including homicides. Rummel attributes most democide to communist regimes, second most to totalitarian and authoritarian ones, and least to democracies. Still fresh in American memories are the Hitlerite holocaust, Stalinist purges, Japanese aggression, and Maoist murders.

William J. Eckhardt and successors calculate that between 1900 and 1995 twentieth century war-related killing totals at least 106,114,000 people, including 62,194,000 civilian and 43,920,000 military victims (Sivard 1996: 19). The continuing slaughter in the "peaceful" period of the "Cold War" between 1945 and 1992 is estimated to be at least 22,057,000 people killed in 149 wars, including 14,505,000 civilians and 7,552,000 combatants (Sivard 1993: 20-1). At least thirty wars were being fought in 1996.

Television screens flash periodically with images of bloodshed from throughout the world, some rooted in ancient animosities and recent atrocities exacerbated by present incapacities to satisfy needs. One horrific crisis follows another as mass media momentarily focus upon one and then move to the next. The bloodshed takes many forms, all rooted in readiness to kill: international wars, civil wars, revolutions, separatist wars, terrorist atrocities, territorial disputes, military coups, genocides, ethno-religious-tribal slaughter, assassinations, foreign interventions, and killing-related mutilations and deprivations. Sometimes foreign antagonisms lead to killing of Americans at home as in the 1993 bombing of the World Trade Center in New York by opponents of United States support for the State of Israel, leaving six dead and one thousand injured. Or killings abroad as in simultaneous truck bombings of American Embassies in Nairobi and Dar Es Salaam in 1998 that left 12 Americans and 300 Africans dead, with some 5,000 injured.

On September 11, 2001, nineteen members of Al-Qaeda, using four hijacked commercial airliners as weapons, carried out suicide attacks on the twin towers of the World Trade Center in New York and the Pentagon in Washington, but did not reach the Capitol, killing 2,986 people. The United States responded with an invasion of Al-Qaeda-based Afghanistan beginning in October 2001 followed by a pre-emptive war on Iraq beginning in March 2003.

Looking out upon the world, American political leaders, echoing Hobbes, are prone to observe, “It’s a jungle out there!” and to commend the maxim of the defunct Roman empire, “If you want peace, prepare for war” (*si vis pacem para bellum*).

* * * * *

In such a context of primal beliefs, philosophical heritage, patriotic socialization, media reinforcement, cultural conditioning, and global bloodshed—it is not surprising that most American political scientists and their students emphatically reject the possibility of a nonkilling society.

When the question is raised in a university setting in the first class meeting from introductory course to graduate seminar the basic objections of human nature, economic scarcity, and necessity to defend against sexual and other assaults customarily appear. Although responses are culturally patterned, variations and extensions are virtually inexhaustible. Each time the question is raised something new can be expected. Human beings are power-seeking, selfish, jealous, cruel and crazy; to kill in self-defense is biologically driven and an inalienable human right. Humans are economically greedy and competitive; social differences and clashing interests make killing inevitable. Other things are worse than killing—psychological abuse and economic deprivation. A nonkilling society would be totalitarian, freedom would be lost; it would be attacked and subjugated by foreign aggressors. Nonkilling as a political principle is immoral; killing to save victims of aggression must always be considered just. Killing criminals for punishment and deterrence benefits society. Weapons cannot be dis-invented; lethal technologies will always exist. No example of a nonkilling society is known in history; it is simply unthinkable.

This is not to imply classroom unanimity. Some American students hold that since humans are capable of creativity and compassion a nonkilling society might be realized through education. Others think that nonkilling conditions might be achieved in small scale societies, but not in large societies and not globally. This is also not to imply that American views are distinctively more violent than those of professors and students of political science in other countries. To find out will require systematic comparative research. But pessimism is probably predominant throughout the present world political science profession.

Yet when the unthinkable question—"Is a nonkilling society possible?"—is asked in other political cultures some surprisingly different answers appear.

I've never thought about the question before . . .

Such is the response of a Swedish colleague at a meeting of Swedish futurists held in Stockholm in 1980 to discuss the idea of a nonviolent political science: "I've never thought about the question before. I need some time to think it over." Surprisingly there is neither automatic rejection nor automatic agreement. The question is taken as needful of reflection and further thought. Similarly, in 1997 at an international meeting of systems scientists in Seoul, a Nobel Laureate in chemistry replies, "I don't know." This is his characteristic reply to questions when an adequate scientific basis for response is absent. He then calls upon members of the conference to take the question seriously since science and civilization advance by questioning the seemingly impossible.

It's thinkable, but . . .

At the XIth World Congress of the International Political Science Association held in Moscow in 1979, two Russian scholars respond to a paper on "Nonviolent Political Science" with qualified willingness to give the question serious consideration. Both surprisingly agree that the goal of politics and political science is the realization of a nonviolent society. "But," one asks, "what is the economic basis of a nonviolent politics and of a nonviolent political science?" "But," asks the other, "how are we to cope with tragedies as in Chile (where a military coup overthrew a democratically elected socialist government), Nicaragua (scene of violent repression and revolution), and

Kampuchea (where more than a million people are killed in revolutionary urban-class extermination)?"

Indeed, what kind of economy neither depends upon nor supports killing—as do contemporary forms of "capitalism" and "communism"? How can nonkilling politics prevent, stop, and remove the lethal aftereffects of murderous atrocities? Under the assumption of nonviolent possibility, questions are raised that are needful of serious scientific inquiry.

We know that human beings are not violent by nature, but . . .

When the question of nonviolent political science is raised with a group of Arab political scientists and public administration scholars at the University of Jordan in Amman in 1981, one professor expressed a collegial consensus: "We know that human beings are not violent by nature." "But," he adds, "we have to fight in self defense." If the primal argument that humans are inescapably violent by nature is questioned, then this opens up the possibility of discovering conditions under which no one kills.

It's not possible, but . . .

During a tenth anniversary seminar held in 1985 at the Institute of Peace Science, Hiroshima University, where mainly Japanese participants divided evenly between those who agreed and disagreed, a professor of education replies, "It's not possible, but it's possible to become possible." While recognizing that a nonkilling society is not immediately realizable, its future feasibility is not dismissed. Then he asks, "What kind of education would be needed to bring about a nonviolent society?" A constructive invitation to creative problem-solving.

It's completely possible . . .

In December 1987 a Korean professor of philosophy, president of the Korean Association of Social Scientists and political leader in Pyongyang, surprisingly replies without hesitation: "It's completely possible." Why? First, humans by nature are not compelled to kill. They are endowed with "consciousness," "reason," and "creativity" that enable them to reject lethality. Second, economic scarcity must not be used to justify killing—men are not the slaves of matter. Scarcity can be overcome by "creativity," "productivity," and "most importantly by equitable distribution." Third, rape should not be used as a basis for rejection of nonkilling. Rape can be eliminated by "education" and "provision of a proper social atmosphere."

In February 2000, when participants in a meeting of some two hundred community leaders in Manizales, Colombia, are asked, "Is a nonkilling society possible?" surprisingly not a single hand is raised to answer no. Then unanimously every hand is raised to affirm yes.

These positive responses in Korea and Colombia are remarkable given the violent contexts of their expression. The violent political traditions of the Democratic People's Republic of Korea parallel in part those of the United States of America: armed anti-colonial revolution, civil war for unification, and righteous defense and offense against domestic and foreign foes. For decades Colombian society has been plagued by the seemingly intractable lethality of military, police, paramilitary, guerrilla, and criminal killers.

Diverse social responses

When the question of the possibility of a nonkilling society is posed without prior discussion in various groups, countries, and cultures, diverse social predispositions to agree or disagree within and across groups are manifested. The promise of systematic global inquiry is made clear.

In Vilnius, Lithuania, at a May 1998 peer review seminar on "New Political Science" composed of political scientists from former Soviet sphere countries, sponsored by the Open Society Institute, eight reply no, one yes. In March 1999 in an introductory political science seminar for graduate students at Seoul National University, twelve respond no, five yes, and two reply yes and no. At a February 1998 forum of Pacific parliamentarians in Honolulu, Hawai'i, organized by the Japan-based Foundation for Support of the United Nations, six answer yes, five no, two respond yes and no. Among an observer group of women from Japan, twelve answer no, eleven yes, and one yes and no.

In Medellín, Colombia, at a November 1998 national conference of educators on the "Future of Education," 275 respond yes, twenty-five no. Among a group of Medellín family social workers, thirty yes, sixteen no. Among a group of young gang members known as *sicarios* (little knives), including hired killers, sixteen answer no, six yes. When asked for reasons for their judgments, a killer says, "I have to kill to take care of my two daughters. There are no jobs." One who answered yes explains, "When the gap between rich and poor closes, we won't have to kill anymore."

In Edmonton, Canada, in October 1997, among a group of high school students convened parallel to a seminar on "Values and the 21st Century" sponsored by the Mahatma Gandhi Canadian Foundation for World Peace, forty-eight reply no, twenty-five yes. In Atlanta, Georgia, at an April 1999 "International Conference on Nonviolence," sponsored by the Martin Luther King, Jr. Center for Nonviolent Social Change, forty answer yes, three no. In Omsk, Russia, in February 2000, among literature students aged seventeen to twenty-six, 121 answer no, 34 yes, and 3 reply yes and no.

* * * * *

Is a nonkilling society possible? Amidst global killing and threats to kill at the violent end of the violent twentieth century, there are understandably ample grounds for political scientists and their students to conclude—It's completely unthinkable! But there are also signs of willingness to give the question serious consideration—It's thinkable and maybe it's possible. Moreover despite unprecedented threats to human survival there are countervailing global resources of spirit, science, institutions, and experience to strengthen confidence that ultimately—It's completely possible.

Chapter 2

CAPABILITIES FOR A NONKILLING SOCIETY

> Already we may know enough for man to close his era of violence if we determine to pursue alternatives.
>
> David N. Daniels and Marshall F. Gilula
>
> Department of Psychiatry, Stanford University, 1970

What are the grounds for thinking that a nonkilling society is possible? Why is it plausible to think that humans are capable of universal respect for life?

Nonkilling Human Nature

Although we might begin with a spiritual basis, first consider a completely secular fact. Most humans do not kill. Of all humans now alive—and of all who have ever lived—only a minority are killers. Consider the homicide statistics of any society.

Consider also killing in war. The world's military and ethnographic museums offer scant evidence that women, half of humankind, have been major combat killers. Granted that women kill, that some have fought in wars and revolutions, that in some societies women and even children have engaged in ritual torture and murder of defeated enemies, and that women are being recruited for killing in several modern armies. But most women have not been warriors or military killers. Add to this the minority combat role of men. Only a minority of men actually fight in wars. Of these only a minority directly kill. Among killers, most experience reluctance and subsequent remorse. Perhaps as few as two percent can kill repeatedly without compunction. As Lieutenant Colonel Dave Grossman explains in a major review of male reluctance to kill in war, "War is an environment that will psychologically debilitate 98 per cent of all who participate in it for any length of time. And the 2 percent who are not driven insane by war appear to have already been insane—aggressive psychopaths—before coming to the battlefield" (Grossman 1995: 50). Thus contrary to the customary political science assumption that humans are natural born killers, the principal task of military training "is to overcome the average individual's deep-seated-resistance to killing" (295).

The human family further evidences nonkilling capability. If human beings are by nature killers, if even half of humanity were inescapably homicidal, then the family in its various forms could not exist. Fathers would kill mothers; mothers, fathers; parents, children; and children, parents. All of these occur but they do not constitute a natural law of lethality that controls the fate of humankind. If it were so, world population long ago would have spiraled into extinction. To the contrary, despite appalling conditions of material deprivation and abuse, the human family has continued to create and sustain life on an unprecedented scale.

A nonkilling global puzzle to challenge ingenuity and evidence for successive attempts at solution is to calculate how many humans have ever lived and how many have and have not been killers. One estimate of total human lives from 1 million B.C.E. to 2000 C.E. is some 91,100,000,000 people (combining Keyfitz 1966 with Weeks 1996: 37, as recalculated by Ramsey 1999). If we inflate Rummel's war and democide deaths to half a billion, assume erroneously that each was killed by a single killer, and arbitrarily multiply by six to account for homicides, we might imagine as many as 3,000,000,000 killers since 1,000 B.C.E. (Figures from 1 million B.C.E. are lacking). But even this crude and inflated estimate of killings would suggest that at least ninety-five percent of humans have not killed. If United States homicide rates were 10 per 100,000 only .01 percent of the population would kill each year. If aggravated assaults were 500 per 100,000 then .5 percent could be added to total .51 percent of the population as actual or attempted killers. Perhaps less than two or even one percent of all homo sapiens have been killers of fellow humans. The percentage of killers in specific societies, of course, may vary greatly according to culture and era (Keeley 1996). Nevertheless the survival and multiplication of humankind testifies to the dominance of vitality over lethality in human nature.

Spiritual Roots

Grounds for confidence in the realizability of a society without killing are present in the spiritual traditions of humankind. Granted that religions have been invoked to justify horrific slaughter from human sacrifice and genocide to atomic annihilation (Thompson 1988). But the principal message of God, the Creator, the Great Spirit, however conceived, has not been "O humankind, hear my Word! Go find another human and kill him or her!" To the contrary it has been "Respect life! Do not kill!"

Nonkilling precepts can be found in all world spiritual faiths. This is why Max Weber deems spiritual commitment to be incompatible with the political imperative to kill. Jainism and Hinduism share the precept of *ahimsa paramo dharma* (nonviolence is the supreme law of life). The first vow of Buddhism is to "abstain from taking life." Judaism, Christianity, and Islam share the divine commandment "Thou shalt not kill" (Exod. 20:13). One of the most ancient Jewish teachings is "Whosoever preserves the life of one person, it is as though he saves a multitude of men. But he who destroys the life of one person, it is as though he destroys the world" (Eisendrath: 144). The core of this teaching, although with qualification, is continued in Islam: "Whosoever kills a human being, except (as punishment) for murder or for spreading corruption in the land, it shall be like killing all humanity; and whosoever saves a life, saves the entire human race" (Al-Qur'an 5:32). The Bahá'í faith—incorporating the teachings of Judaism, Christianity, and Islam—enjoins "Fear God, O people, and refrain from shedding the blood of anyone" (Bahá'u'lláh 1983: 277).

Humanist traditions also hold forth the desirability and possibility of a nonkilling society. In Confucianism, when morality among rulers prevails, no death penalty will be needed (Fung 1952: 60). In Taoism, when humans live simply, spontaneously, and in harmony with nature, "although there might exist weapons of war, no one will drill with them" (Fung 1952: 190). In modern socialist thought when workers refuse to support killing each other, wars will cease. An anti-WWI manifesto proclaims:

> All class conscious members of the Industrial Workers of the World are conscientiously opposed to shedding the life blood of human beings, not for religious reasons, as are the Quakers and Friendly Societies, but because we believe that the interests and welfare of the working class in all are identical. While we are bitterly opposed to the Imperialist Capitalist Government of Germany we are against slaughtering and maiming the workers of any country. (True 1995: 49; for a courageous example, see Baxter 2000).

In all societies murder is disapproved. Humanist respect parallels religious reverence for life.

What significance does the presence of a nonkilling ethic in world spiritual and humanist traditions have for the realizability of nonkilling societies? On the one hand it reveals divine intent to plant profound respect for life in the consciousness of humankind. On the other, it demonstrates human capacity to receive, respond to, or to create such a principle. If humans are incurably killers by nature, neither reception, nor transmission, nor creation of such a principle would be plausible. Even if a nonkilling spiritual ethic were invented by elites to discourage revolution, by the oppressed to weaken oppressors, or by killers to escape retribution it implies that humans to whom it is addressed are capable of responding positively to it.

The spirit of nonkilling has emerged before, during, and after history's most horrible outbreaks of bloodshed. Its expression is not just a luxury benevolently bestowed by killers. Irrepressibly surviving into the contemporary era, it continues to inspire liberation from lethality in post-crusades Christianity, post-conquest Islam, post-Holocaust Judaism, post-militarist Buddhism, and post-colonial traditions of indigenous peoples. In the murderous twentieth century it can be seen in courageous contributions to nonviolent global change by the Christians Tolstoy and Martin Luther King, Jr., the Hindu Gandhi, the Muslim Abdul Ghaffar Khan, the Jew Joseph Abileah, the Buddhist Dalai Lama, the Green Petra Kelly, and countless others, celebrated and unsung.

The presence of the nonkilling spirit in each faith and examples of principled commitments to it open the way for awakening and affirmation by hundreds of millions of co-believers. Dissonant tension between the nonkilling imperative and recognition of responsibility for killing and its noxious consequences creates motivation for nonkilling personal and social change. While roots of nonkilling can be found within each tradition, the spiritual heritage of humankind as a whole is like the multiple root system that sustains the life of a banyan tree. Inspiration and sustenance can be drawn from the entire root system as well as from any part of it. For all tap the power of life. The reality of respect for life in religious and humanist faiths provides a strong spiritual basis for confidence that a nonkilling global society is possible.

Scientific Roots

"We will never get to nonviolence by religion alone." Such is the advice of one of India's foremost religious leaders, Acharya Mahapragya, creative inheritor of the ancient Jain tradition of *ahimsa* (nonviolence). In Jain thought, "Ahimsa is the heart of all stages of life, the core of all sacred texts, and the sum . . . and substance . . . of all vows and virtues" (Jain and Varni 1993: 139). For Acharya Mahapragya, the way to realize a nonviolent society is to empower individuals to discover nonviolence within themselves and to express it socially by combining modern neuroscience with spiritual truths. In his analysis, violence is caused by emotions produced by the endocrine glands affecting the sympathetic and parasympathetic nervous systems and is related to what we eat. Furthermore based upon scientific knowledge of our neurological system we can purposively use the energy of our brains in simple meditational practices to nurture nonviolence within and to commit ourselves to nonviolent social life (Mahaprajna (sic) 1987 and 1994; Zaveri and Kumar 1992).

What are some scientific grounds for confidence in nonkilling human capabilities? By science is meant broadly all forms of knowledge gained by questioning and experimentation—facts, theories, and methods for determining validity and reliability. A harbinger of scientific revolution is when some philosophers begin to question accepted thinking.

This has been done for nonviolence by A. Richard Konrad (1974) who questions the conventional assumption that readiness to kill is the only effective way to cope with violence from rape to holocaust. Konrad argues that the thesis of the single violent problem-solving alternative rests upon three assumptions: that all nonviolent alternatives have been identified; that all have been tried; and that all have failed. But these assumptions are untenable: nonviolent problem-solving alternatives are hypothetically infinite; practical constraints of time, resources, and other factors prevent testing even those that are identified; therefore we cannot be certain that the single violent alternative is the only one that can succeed. Thus Konrad argues the need to shift from a philosophical predisposition to accept violence to one that seeks to create and test nonviolent alternatives. Such an approach is likely to lead to scientific discoveries that question the inescapability of human lethality. (See also Yoder 1983).

The assumption that humans must inevitably be killers because of their animal nature is being questioned. Tulane University psychologist Loh Tseng Tsai (1963) has demonstrated that a rat-killing cat and a sewer rat can be taught to eat peacefully out of the same dish. The method was a combination of operant conditioning and social learning. At first separated by a glass partition, the two animals learned that they must simultaneously press parallel levers to release food pellets into a common feeding dish. After seven hundred training sessions the partition could be removed without bloodshed.

Tsai concludes:

> We have demonstrated for the first time in the history of science with crucial experiments that cats and rats—the so-called natural enemies—can and do cooperate. Such a discovery throws overboard the traditional dogma in psychology that in animal nature there is an ineradicable instinct of pugnacity which makes fighting or wars inevitable (1963: 4).

Observing that "many think that our research has laid the cornerstone of the basic biological foundation for the theoretical possibility of world peace," Tsai calls for a science-based philosophy of "survival through cooperation" rather than continuation of the presumed inescapability of competitive lethality. In a radically different field, the physicist and historian of science Antonino Drago, contrasting the implications of Carnotian versus Newtonian mechanics for conflict resolution, arrives at a similar science-based recommendation in favor of transcendent cooperation (Drago 1994). So does the psychotherapist Jerome D. Frank in recommending cooperation toward mutually beneficial common goals to overcome deadly antagonisms (Frank 1960: 261–2; 1993: 204–5).

Challenge to the assumption that human lethality is inescapably rooted in our evolutionary emergence as a species of "killer ape" comes from new studies of a genetically almost identical primate species—the nonkilling bonobo of Central Africa (Kano 1990). The Mangandu people of the Congo, who share the tropical forest with the bonobo, strictly prohibit killing them based on a legend that once their ancestors and the bonobo lived together as kin (Kano 1990: 62). In contrast to gorillas, chimpanzees, and other apes, bonobo have not been observed to kill each other (Wrangham and Peterson, 1990; Waal 1997). Furthermore, recent studies of "peacemaking" and "reciprocal altruism" among primate species who do kill also call into question the tendency to claim only lethality but not nonkilling potentiality in evolutionary human nature (Waal 1989; 1996). There is a peaceful side of animal nature and, as Kropotkin (1914), Sorokin (1954), and Alfie Kohn (1990) have demonstrated, a cooperative, altruistic, and "brighter side" of human nature as well.

In a comparative study of aggression in animals and humans, the ethologist-anthropologist Irenäus Eibl-Eibesfeldt (1979: 240–1) finds that there is a biological basis for the spiritual imperative not to kill. Observing that "in many animal species intraspecific aggression is so ritualized that it does not result in physical harm," he finds similar and more elaborate human techniques for avoiding bloodshed. “To some extent,” he concludes, “a biological norm filter lays down the commandment: ‘Thou shalt not kill.’” But “in the course of cultural pseudospeciation (defining others as not fully human and thus subject to predation), man has superimposed a cultural norm filter that commands him to kill upon his biological norm filter, which forbids him to kill.” In war, “this leads to a conflict of norms of which man is aware through the conscience that pricks him as soon as he apprehends the enemy and confronts him as a human being.” This is evidenced by post-killing warrior needs for purification and social acceptance.

Confirming Eibl-Eibesfeldt’s thesis is Grossman’s finding that “throughout history the majority of men on the battlefield would not attempt to kill the enemy, even to save their own lives or the lives of their friends” (Grossman 1995: 4). Grossman notes that psychiatric casualties among soldiers who have killed directly are higher than nonkillers. The soldier-psychologist and the ethologist-anthropologist differ only on the policy implications of their findings. For the former the task is to provide professional training to overcome resistance to killing. For the latter the problem is to bring culture into conformance with nonkilling human biology. Eibl-Eibesfeldt concludes:

> The root of the universal desire for peace lies in this conflict between cultural and biological norms, which makes men want to bring their biological and cultural norm filters into accord. Our conscience remains our hope, and based on this, a rationally guided evolution could lead to peace. This presupposes recognition of the fact that war performs functions that will have to be performed some other way, without bloodshed. (1979: 241).

Brain science provides further support for confidence in nonkilling human potential. Terming his approach “Neurorealism,” the pioneering neuro-scientist Bruce E. Morton

(2000) presents a "Dual Quadbrain Model of Behavioral Laterality" that describes the neurobiological bases of both nonkilling and killing. The four parts of the model "function in two modes of a single tetradic system." They are the brain core system (instincts), the limbic system (emotions), the right and left hemisphere systems (imagination and intellect), and the neocerebellar system (intuition). Morton locates the source of higher spiritual and social consciousness in the system of neocerebellar intuition. This "Higher Source" is "truthful, creative, self-disciplined, altruistic, cooperative, empathic, and nonviolent." It facilitates the long-term survival of the group and is "strictly a brain dependent phenomenon accessible to all. The emergence of the "Source" into consciousness can be evoked in three ways: by near-death trauma, by certain hallucinogenic drugs, and most importantly by meditation. In everyday social life, the "Source" intuitively facilitates the emergent benefits of synergy "toward nonviolent community." It benefits from and contributes to the absence of lethal threats to survival.

Thus neurorealist brain science provides a basis for self-activated nonviolent commitment and social transformation that is entirely consistent with nonkilling spirituality and biological reluctance to kill. It is also compatible with the Hindu Vivekananda's insight that the task of the great religious teachers is not to bring God from outside but to assist each person to bring out preexisting godliness within. It resonates with the Christian Tolstoy's affirmation that "the kingdom of God is within you" (Tolstoy 1974). Compare the insight of the fifteenth century Indian mystic Kabir:

> Between the two eyes is the Master,
> The messenger of the Lord.
> Within your own body resides your Lord,
> Why open the outer eyes to look for Him?
> (Sethi 1984: 56-7)

But suppose biology-based brain dysfunctions predispose some individuals to be compulsive killers? Even if such lethality is biologically driven and not produced by conditioning and culture, scientific ingenuity promises to empower pathological killers to liberate themselves from compulsion to kill. And to do so without impairing other human qualities. With the rise of modern neuroscience, genetics, and other biosciences, the inescapable lethality of "human nature," even if connected to atypical biological impairment, can no longer be assumed.

A pioneering example is provided by the basic and applied research of the developmental neuropsychologist James W. Prescott and the neuropsychiatrist Robert G. Heath (Restak 1979: 118–133). They theorize that compulsion to kill by some individuals is related to impairment of the electrical circuits ("pleasure pathways") connecting areas of the brain that connect emotions (limbic system) and bodily movement (cerebellum). They further hypothesize that promotion or impairment of these circuits is related to degree of circular bodily movement in early childhood development, testing this by raising chimpanzees with heads immobilized in a vise or by twirling them around in a swivel chair. Subsequently, they found the restrained chimpanzees to be more aggressive and the mobile ones to be more social. Proceeding to human application on institutionalized killers, they implanted a small electrode in the hind brain that can be self-controlled by a pocket stimulator operating through a device implanted in the homicidally compulsive person's shoulder ("cerebellar stimulator" or "cerebellar pacemaker"). When a feeling of dysphoria and the urge to kill arises, the person can activate the pleasure pathways to remove it. Some individuals diagnosed as "criminally insane" have experienced immediate relief after years of solitary confinement or restraint. Others have experienced gradual disappearance of homicidal and suicidal urges. There have been failures. In one case the cerebellar wire broke and the patient immediately killed a nurse with a pair of scissors. Nevertheless the successes of this pioneering procedure challenge new theoretical and technological innovations to liberate humankind from lethal biological pessimism.

Further grounds for nonkilling optimism—contrasting sharply with political science pessimism—are found in the conclusions of twenty-three Stanford University psychiatrists who formed a committee to study the "crisis of violence" in the United States following the assassinations of Martin Luther King, Jr. and Senator Robert F. Kennedy (Daniels, Gilula, and Ochberg 1970). After reviewing violence and aggression in relation to biology, psychodynamics, environment, anger, intergroup conflict, mass media, firearms, mental illness, drug use, and other factors Daniels and Gilula conclude: "*Already we may know enough for man to close his era of violence if we determine to pursue alternatives*" (emphasis added) (441).

Case studies of homicide presented by psychiatrist George F. Solomon (1970) make killing understandable and plausibly preventable in contrast to helpless reference to "human nature." In one case, the socialization experience of a seemingly unemotional, random sniper-killer of women included: parental neglect by his gambling father, seduction by his alcoholic and promiscuous mother, fascination with guns, and drug use to block out "horrible images" of incestuous guilt. In another case, the background of a killer of his ex-wife's new husband included: poverty, hatred of father for violence against his mother, convulsion after a paternal beating on the head, maternal ridicule, being beaten by his sisters, becoming a first sergeant in the Marine Corps, marriage to a prostitute met in a brothel, fathering two children by her, assault upon her and slashing his own wrists after discovering her infidelity while he was on duty overseas, being threatened by her with a .38 caliber handgun, and possession of his service pistol with which he killed—not her—but her new husband amidst a three-sided, living room quarrel about child support and visitation rights.

Solomon concludes:

> As a psychiatrist I have a firm commitment to the idea that human behavior can be modified. Our failures in prevention and treatment have been based on ignorance, which can be ameliorated through further research; on lack of implementation of accepted principles; on a reluctance to innovate; and on a vindictiveness toward social deviancy far more than any intrinsic "incurability" of the violence-prone person. The human's capacity for growth and healing is great and, hopefully, his proclivity for violence can be halted (387).

In anthropology, new interest in understanding human capacities for nonviolence and peace as contrasted with customary emphasis upon violence and aggression is producing knowledge to question the assumption that a nonkilling society is impossible (Sponsel and Gregor 1994b; Sponsel 1996). As Leslie E. Sponsel explains, "Nonviolent and peaceful societies appear to be rare—not because they are, in fact, rare but because nonviolence and peace are too rarely considered in research, the media, and other areas." He adds, "It is as important to understand the characteristics, conditions, causes, functions, processes, and consequences of nonviolence and peace as it is to understand those of violence and war" (Sponsel 1994a: 18–9).

Scientific questioning of the Hobbesian assumption of universal lethality among early humans has been advanced by Piero Giorgi (1999) and J.M.G. van der Dennen (1990; 1995). In a review of evidence for war and feuding for 50,000 "primitive" peoples recorded in the ethnographic literature over the past century, van der Dennen finds explicit confirmation for only 2,000 groups. Acknowledging that absence of information about "belligerence" for the remaining groups does not necessarily prove their peacefulness, van der Dennen cautions against dogmatic acceptance of the assumption of universal human bellicosity (1990: 257, 259, 264-9). He cites ethnographic evidence for 395 "highly unwarlike" peoples from Aboriginals to Zuni (1995: 595–619).

Reviewing the anthropological literature, Bruce D. Bonta (1993) identifies forty-seven societies that demonstrate human capacities for "peacefulness."

> Peacefulness . . . is defined as a condition whereby people live with a relatively high degree of interpersonal harmony; experience little physical violence among adults, between adults and children, and between the sexes; have developed workable strategies for resolving conflicts and averting violence; are committed to avoiding violence (such as warfare) with other peoples; raise their children to adopt peaceful ways; and have a strong consciousness of themselves as peaceful (4).

Bonta finds evidence of peacefulness among the Amish, Anabaptists, Balinese, Batek, Birhor, Brethren, Buid, Chewong, Doukhobors, Fipa, Fore, G/wi, Hutterites, Ifaluk, Inuit, Jains, Kadar, !Kung, Ladakhis, Lepchas, Malapandaram, Mbuti, Mennonites, Montagnais-Naskapi, Moravians, Nayaka, Nubians, Onge, Orang Asli, Paliyan, Piaroa, Quakers, Rural Northern Irish, Rural Thai, San, Sanpoil, Salteaux, Semai, Tahitians, Tanka, Temiar, Toraja, Tristan Islanders, Waura, Yanadi, Zapotec, and Zuni.

In a further study of conflict resolution among twenty-four of these peoples, Bonta (1996) concludes:

> Several common notions about conflict and conflict resolution that are asserted by Western scholars can be questioned in light of the success of these societies in peacefully resolving conflicts: namely, that violent conflict is inevitable in all societies;

> that punishment and armed force prevent internal and external violence; that political structures are necessary to prevent conflicts; and that conflict should be viewed as positive and necessary. The contrary evidence is that over half of the peaceful societies have no recorded violence; they rarely punish adults (except for the threat of ostracism); they handle conflicts with outside societies in the same peaceful ways that they approach internal conflicts; they do not look to outside governments when they have internal disputes; and they have a highly negative view of conflict (403).

A recurrent anthropological finding is the importance of child socialization and community self-identity among other factors differentiating societies high or low in violence (Fabbro 1978). Their significance is shown in a comparative study by Douglas P. Fry (1994) of two Mexican Zapotec villages of similar socio-economic characteristics but markedly different in incidence of violence. In peaceful La Paz, where homicide is rare, citizens see themselves as "respectful, peaceful, nonjealous, and cooperative" (140). In nearby violent San Andrés, there is a "widely held countervailing belief or value system that condones violence" (141). This is accompanied by lack of respect for women, wife-beatings, physical punishment of children, disobedient children, swearing, drunken brawling, and killing in sexual rivalries, feuds, and revenge. With material and structural conditions much the same, the homicide rate in San Andrés is 18.1 per 100,000 compared with 3.4 in La Paz. This comparison helps us to understand that pessimism about human nature and community norms condoning violence are correlated with killing; whereas nonviolent beliefs and values predispose to a nonkilling society.

Major scientific support for confidence in nonkilling human capabilities is provided by the historic Seville "Statement on Violence" on May 16, 1986 issued by an international group of specialists in the disciplines of animal behavior, behavior genetics, biological anthropology, ethology, neurophysiology, physical anthropology, political psychology, psychiatry, psychobiology, psychology, social psychology, and sociology.[2] They declare:

> IT IS SCIENTIFICALLY INCORRECT to say that we have inherited the tendency to make war from our animal ancestors . . . . IT IS SCIENTIFICALLY INCORRECT to say that war or any other violent behaviour is genetically programmed into our human nature . . . . IT IS SCIENTIFICALLY INCORRECT to say that in the course of human evolution there has been a selection of aggressive behavior more than for other kinds of behavior . . . . IT IS SCIENTIFICALLY INCORRECT to say that humans have a "violent brain" . . . . IT IS SCIENTIFICALLY INCORRECT to say that war is caused by 'instinct' or any single motivation.

Paralleling nonkilling optimism of the Stanford psychiatrists, the Seville scientists declare:

> We conclude that biology does not condemn humanity to war, and that humanity can be freed from the bondage of biological pessimism and empowered with confidence to undertake the transformative tasks needed in this International Year of Peace and in the years to come. Although these tasks are institutional and collective, they also rest upon the consciousness of individual participants for whom pessimism and optimism are crucial factors. Just as 'wars begin in the minds of men,' peace also begins in our minds. The same species who invented war is capable of inventing peace. The responsibility lies with each of us (Adams 1989: 120–1; 1997).

On August 2, 1939 Albert Einstein wrote a letter to President Franklin D. Roosevelt informing him that atomic physics had advanced to a point where creation of "extremely powerful bombs of a new type" was "conceivable" (Nathan and Norden, 1968: 295). This resulted in formation of an advisory committee, an initial United States Government investment of six thousand dollars, the organization of the multi-billion dollar Manhattan Project, and the creation and use six years later of the world's first uranium and plutonium bombs. Sixty years later it is possible to assert that there is enough emerging scientific evidence of nonviolent human capabilities which—if systematically integrated and advanced—holds forth the possibility of empowering nonkilling human self-transformation. Among indicators are more than one hundred doctoral dissertations reporting research on "nonviolence" that increasingly have appeared since 1963 in the United States alone in such fields as anthropology, education, history, language and literature, philosophy, psychology, political science, religion, sociology, speech, and theology (*Dissertation Abstracts International* 1963-)

Adding research completed in other countries such as India, in languages other than English, in papers presented in academic conferences, in books and interdisciplinary symposia (Kool 1990; 1993), in pioneering integrative analyses (Gregg 1966), in new journals (*International Journal of Nonviolence* 1993–), in a major annotated bibliographic survey of nonviolent action (McCarthy and Sharp 1997), and in other sources—it is clear that a substantial body of nonviolent knowledge is growing in addition to the literature on "peace" and "conflict resolution." Present nonviolent knowledge potential is functionally comparable to the state of atomic physics in 1939.

Salient Outcroppings of Nonkilling Capability

Emile Durkheim (1858–1917), a founder of modern sociology, urged attention to "salient outcroppings" of social life related to questions of theoretical interest. This idea is carried forward by the American social psychologist Donald T. Campbell who taught Northwestern University political science graduate students to be alert to observe "naturally occurring social experiments" akin to those that might be contrived in an experimental laboratory (Paige 1971). Since political science is prone to develop theory out of observing practice—such as in Machiavelli's theoretical elaboration of the techniques of ruthless ruler Cesare Borgia in *The Prince*—examples of nonkilling behavior arising "naturally" out of historical and contemporary experience are especially significant for recognizing possibilities for nonviolent social change.

Among salient manifestations of nonkilling capabilities are public policies, institutions, cultural expressions, nonviolent political struggles, historical examples, and dedicated individuals.

Public policies. Remarkable examples of political decisions tending toward realization of nonkilling societies are found in countries that have abolished the death penalty, countries that have no armies, and countries that recognize the right of conscientious objection to killing in military service.

By April 2006, eighty-seven of 196 world countries and territories had abolished the death penalty for all crimes.

TABLE 2

COUNTRIES AND TERRITORIES WITHOUT DEATH PENALTY (87)

ANDORRA	GREECE	PALAU
ANGOLA	GUINEA-BISSAU	PANAMA
ARMENIA	HAITI	PARAGUAY
AUSTRALIA	HONDURAS	PHILIPPINES
AUSTRIA	HUNGARY	POLAND
AZERBAIJAN	ICELAND	PORTUGAL
BELGIUM	IRELAND	ROMANIA
BHUTAN	ITALY	SAMOA
BOZNIA-HERZGOVINA	KIRIBATI	SAN MARINO
BULGARIA	LIBERIA	SAO TOMÉ AND PRINCIPE
CAMBODIA	LIECHTENSTEIN	SENEGAL
CANADA	LITHUANIA	SERBIA AND MONTENEGRO
CAPE VERDE	LUXEMBOURG	SEYCHELLES
COLOMBIA	MACEDONIA	SLOVAK REPUBLIC
COSTA RICA	MALTA	SLOVENIA
COTE D'IVOIRE	MARSHALL	SOLOMON ISLANDS
CROATIA	MAURITIUS	SOUTH AFRICA
CYPRUS	MEXICO	SPAIN
CZECH REPUBLIC	MICRONESIA	SWEDEN
DENMARK	MOLDOVA	SWITZERLAND
DJIBOUTI	MONACO	TURKMENISTAN
DOMINICAN REPUBLIC	MOZAMBIQUE	TURKEY
EAST TIMOR	NAMIBIA	TUVALU
ECUADOR	NEPAL	UKRAINE
ESTONIA	NETHERLANDS	UNITED KINGDOM
FINLAND	NEW ZEALAND	URUGUAY
FRANCE	NICARAGUA	VANUATU
GEORGIA	NIUE	VATICAN CITY STATE
GERMANY	NORWAY	VENEZUELA

Amnesty International, August 2006.

Each instance of complete abolition of capital punishment is of compelling scientific and public policy interest. Why, how, and when did each government decide not to kill? Why are some countries, cultures, and regions represented while others are conspicuously absent? What historical processes of innovation and diffusion account for the present global pattern? And what implications do these examples of nonviolent change have for future universal realization of societies without killing?

In addition to the completely abolitionist countries, eleven states have abolished the death penalty for ordinary crimes while retaining it for special circumstances of martial law or war (for example, Argentina, Brazil, Cook Islands, Israel, Latvia, and Peru). Twenty-nine states retain the death penalty in law but had not executed anyone for ten or more years (for example, Algeria, Brunei Darussalam, Congo (Republic), Papua New Guinea, Russian Federation, and Tunisia). Sixty-nine countries retain the death penalty in law and continue to kill (including China, Egypt, India, Indonesia, Japan, Nigeria, Pakistan, Rwanda, and the United States). While the United States retains the death penalty for federal crimes, twelve of its fifty states and the District of Columbia have abolished it: Alaska, Hawai'i, Iowa, Maine, Massachusetts, Michigan, Minnesota, North Dakota, Rhode Island, Vermont, West Virginia, and Wisconsin.

Despite oscillations between rejection and reimposition, the global trend toward abolition of the death penalty by governments emerging from traditions of violence reinforces confidence in the attainability of nonkilling societies. Killing of citizens need not be part of Rosseau's "social contract" nor an inalienable attribute of politics as prescribed by Max Weber.

Consider also countries without armies, twenty-seven in 2001. All are members of the United Nations except the Cook Islands, Niue, and the Vatican.

TABLE 3

COUNTRIES WITHOUT ARMIES (27)

No Army (19)	No Army (Defense Treaty) (8)
Costa Rica	Andorra (Spain, France)
Dominica	Cook Islands (New Zealand)
Grenada	Iceland (NATO, USA)
Haiti	Marshall Islands (USA)
Kiribati	Micronesia (USA)
Liechtenstein	Monaco (France)
Maldives	Niue (New Zealand)
Mauritius	Palau (USA)
Nauru	
Panama	
Saint Kitts and Nevis	
Saint Lucia	
Saint Vincent and the Grenadines	
Samoa	
San Marino	
Solomon Islands	
Tuvalu	
Vanuatu	
Vatican	

Source: Barbey 2001.

In addition, at least eighteen dependent territories or geographical regions are demilitarized by agreement with the sovereignty-claiming country such as the Aland Islands of Finland, or by international treaty, including Antarctica and the Moon (Barbey 2001).

The absence of armies may be surprising in countries where they are deemed to be indispensable for national identity, social control, defense, and offense. But even though countries without armies are small—and although some are qualified by dependence upon armed allies or by presence of para-military forces—they demonstrate the possibility of nonmilitary statehood. Nonkilling nations are not unthinkable.

In countries that do have armies, state recognition of conscientious objection to military conscription provides further evidence of nonkilling political potential. Forty-seven countries in 1998 recognized in law some form of principled refusal by citizens to kill in military service.

TABLE 4

COUNTRIES AND TERRITORIES RECOGNIZING CONSCIENTIOUS OBJECTION TO MILITARY SERVICE (47)

Australia	Lithuania
Austria	Malta
Azerbaijan	Moldova
Belgium	Netherlands
Bermuda	Norway
Brazil	Paraguay
Bulgaria	Poland
Canada	Portugal
Croatia	Romania
Cyprus (Greek-Cyprus)	Russia
Czech Republic	Slovakia
Denmark	Slovenia
Estonia	South Africa
Finland	Spain
France	Suriname
Germany	Sweden
Greece	Switzerland
Guyana	Ukraine
Hungary	United Kingdom
Israel	United States
Italy	Uruguay
Kyrgyzstan	Uzbekistan
Latvia	Yugoslavia
	Zimbabwe

Source: Horeman and Stolwijk 1998

Acceptable legal grounds for objection vary widely from narrow religious requirements to broad recognition of spiritual, philosophical, ethical, moral, humanitarian, or political reasons for refusal to kill. Also varying widely are requirements for alternative service, ability of soldiers already in service to claim conscientious objection, and degree of reliability in implementation of the laws (Moskos and Chambers 1993). The most liberal current nonkilling right is contained in Article 4 of the Basic Law of 1949 in the Federal Republic of Germany: "No one shall be forced to do war service with arms against his conscience" (Kuhlmann and Lippert 1993: 98). As is the case with abolition of the death penalty and the emergence of countries without armies, the origins, processes, global patterning, and prospects for political recognition of refusal to serve as military killers is of surpassing scientific interest.

Social Institutions

Institutions approximating those appropriate in or functional for transition to future nonkilling societies already have appeared in various parts of the world. They provide further evidence of human capacity for commitment not to kill. If these scattered institutions were creatively combined and adapted to the needs of any single society, it is even now plausible to envision a society without killing that is not the product of hypothetical speculation but is based upon demonstrated human experience. Of the many, a few are briefly mentioned here. Each has a story that merits telling in full.

Spiritual institutions. Religious institutions inspired by nonkilling faiths can be found throughout the world. Among them are the Jains of the East, Quakers of the West, the Universal Peace and Brotherhood Association of Japan, the Buddhist Plum Village community in France, the Simon Kimbangu Church in Africa, the Doukhobor (Spirit Wrestler) pacifists of Russia and Canada, and the Jewish Peace Fellowship in the United States. Globally the International Fellowship of Reconciliation, founded in 1919, brings together men and women of every faith "who, from the basis of a belief in the power of love and truth to create justice and restore community, commit themselves to active nonviolence as a way of life and as a means of transformation—personal, social, economic, and political."

Political institutions. An electoral political party committed to principled nonviolence is the Fellowship Party of Britain, founded by Ronald Mallone, John Loverseed, and other Christian pacifists and WWII veterans in 1955.[3] It campaigns against all preparations for war, and for economic and social justice, while celebrating the arts and sports. In Germany, "nonviolence" is asserted among the salient values of the ecological Die Grünen (Green Party) founded by Petra K. Kelly and thirty others in 1979.[4] Among sources of inspiration were the nonviolent movements associated with Gandhi and Martin Luther King, Jr. (Kelly 1989). Although uncertainly salient in policy practice as Green parties diffuse throughout the world, the founding commitment to nonviolence by an innovative social movement-electoral party provides a significant political precedent. The United States Pacifist Party, founded in 1983 on spiritual, scientific, and humanist principles by Bradford Lyttle, who became its candidate in the presidential elections of 1996 and 2000, seeks nonviolent transformation of American society and its role in the world.[5] In India, the Sarvodaya Party, founded by T.K.N. Unnithan and others, enters the electoral arena to promote the Gandhian model of social development for the well-being of all.[6] Justifying its break with the Gandhian tradition of remaining aloof from politics, the Sarvodaya Party explains: "Power is neutral in character, it becomes corrupting only in the hands of a corrupt people." At a global level, the unique Transnational Radical Party, inspired by Gandhian nonviolence, has emerged out of Italy's Partito Radicale in 1987.[7] Its purpose is to work exclusively at the international level to exert nonviolent influence upon the United Nations; for example, for worldwide abolition of the death penalty, for recognition of conscientious objection, and for prosecution of war criminals. The party does not contest national elections; members may hold dual membership in any party; and dues are prorated at one percent of the gross national product per capita of member countries. Under Gandhi's image the party proclaims: "Transnational law and nonviolence are the most effective and radical ways to build a better world."

Economic institutions. Salient economic institutions that express nonkilling principles include a capitalist mutual stock fund that will not invest in war industries (Pax World Fund); a labor union inspired by Gandhian and Kingian nonviolence (United Farm Workers of America founded by Cesar Chavez, Dolores Heurta, and others); and a comprehensive community development program in Sri Lanka based upon nonviolent Buddhist principles (the Sarvodaya Shramadana Sangamaya, led by A.T. Ariyaratne). Although limited in success, the experience of India's *bhoodan* (land gift) movement to transfer land to the landless—inspired by Gandhi's theory of "trusteeship" and led by Vinoba Bhave (1994) and Jayaprakash Narayan (1978)—has demonstrated that nonviolent sharing of scarce resources is not unthinkable. Philanthropic foundations support nonviolent service to society: The Gandhi Foundation (London), the Savodaya International Trust (Bangalore), and the A.J. Muste Institute (New York).

Educational institutions. The possibility of basing an entire university upon the multifaith spirit of nonviolence in service to human needs has been bequeathed by the inspired Gandhian educator Dr. G. Ramachandran (1903–1995), founder of Gandhigram Rural Institute (Deemed University) in Tamil Nadu, India. Serving thirty surrounding villages, some of the University's important founding features were: (1) combining disciplinary studies and community applications; political science and village decision-making, physics and radio repair, biology and well-cleaning, arts and creative child development, (2) requiring problem-solving theses by every graduating student, (3) teaching trilingual language competence with Tamil for local needs, Hindi for national integration, and English as a window on the world, and (4) engaging all in labor for campus maintenance and services; without, for example, janitors, grounds keepers, and cooks.

Ramachandran's distinctive contribution was to establish within this institution of higher education a nonviolent alternative to military training—a Shanti Sena (Peace Corps)—whose dynamic chief organizer became humanities professor N. Radhakrishnan (1992; 1997). From 1958 to 1988 the Shanti Sena trained five thousand voluntarily disciplined and uniformed young men and women who pledged "to work for peace and to be prepared, if need be, to lay down my life for it." Combining spiritual, physical, intellectual, and organizational training, the Shanti Sena prepared students for conflict resolution, security functions, disaster relief, and cooperative community service in response to community needs. The approach was always to work *together with* villagers to improve such things as childcare, sanitation, housing, and preservation of folk arts traditions. While in the mid-1970s some urban universities in India were firebombed as instruments of oppression, villagers around Gandhigram held festivals to celebrate elevation of their Rural Institute to the status of Deemed University. The Shanti Sena assumed responsibility for campus security. No armed police were permitted on campus, even during visits by Indian prime ministers Nehru, Indira Gandhi, and other dignitaries.

Training institutions. Institutions that provide nonviolence training for social change, conflict zone interventions, social defense, and other purposes are rapidly appearing. Experienced trainers are increasingly in demand within and across national boundaries and are contributing to growing confidence in human ability to replace violent means with nonviolent methods of problem-solving. To note a few organizations and prominent trainers (Beer 1994): the G. Ramachandran School of Nonviolence (N. Radhakrishnan), Peace Brigades International (Narayan Desai), Florida Martin Luther King, Jr. Institute for Nonviolence with LaFayette & Associates (Bernard LaFayette, Jr., Charles L. Alphin, Sr., and David Jehnsen), International Fellowship of Reconciliation (Hildegaard Goss-Mayr and Richard Deats), Training Center Workshops (George Lakey), War Resisters International (Howard Clark), Palestinian Center for the Study of Nonviolence (Mubarak Awad), Nonviolence International (Michael Beer), Servicio Paz y Justicia (Adolfo Pèrez Esquivel), the International Network of Engaged Buddhists (Yeshua Moser-Puangsuwan), and TRANSCEND (Johan Galtung).

An important resource for training in nonviolent personal defense and character development with profound implications for extrapolation into nonviolent strategic social change is the creative nonkilling martial art Aikido, originating in Japan. As taught by its founder, Morihei Ueshiba, "To smash, injure, or destroy is the worse sin a human can commit." The objective of Aikido is harmony with the life force of the universe. "Aikido is the manifestation of love" (Stevens 1987: 94, 112; Yoder 1983: 28).

Security institutions. Several institutions throughout the world illustrate capacity to seek community security by nonlethal means. Among them are found countries with virtually unarmed citizenry (Japan), police virtually without firearms (Britain), a prison without armed guards (Finland), unarmed zones of peace (Sitio Cantomanyog, Philippines), an association for unarmed civilian defense (Bund für Soziale Verteidigung, Minden, Germany), and nonviolent organizations that carry out peacemaking interventions in combat zones (Moser-

Puangsuwan and Weber 2000; Mahony and Eguren 1997). To these must be added the various movements by governments and citizen organizations in the direction of a weapon-free world: to abolish nuclear, biological, and chemical weapons; and to ban handguns, assault weapons, and land mines. Among organizations are the Center for Peace and Reconciliation, founded by former Costa Rican president and 1987 Nobel peace laureate Oscar Arias Sánchez for demilitarization and conflict resolution; the Movement to Abolish the Arms Trade, emulating anti-slave trade experience; and Nature/Gunless Society, founded in the Philippines by Reynaldo Pacheco and Haydee Y. Yorac, dedicated to saving human beings as an "endangered species" (Villavincensio-Paurom 1995).

Research institutions. In the West, The Albert Einstein Institution (Cambridge, Massachusetts), founded by Gene Sharp, carries out research on nonviolent struggles for democracy, security, and justice throughout the world. In the East, the Gandhian Institute of Studies (Varanasi, India), founded by Jayaprakash ("J.P.") Narayan, conducts social science research to support nonviolent social change. At the transnational level, the Nonviolence Commission of the International Peace Research Association founded by Theodore L. Herman promotes worldwide sharing of discoveries in research, education, and action.

Problem-solving institutions. Examples of institutions dedicated to solving problems on nonkilling principles include Amnesty International (defense of human rights and abolition of the death penalty), Greenpeace International (defense of the environment and abolition of nuclear weapons), the War Resisters International (defense of conscientious objection to military conscription and resistance to all preparations for war), and Médicins sans Frontières (humanitarian medical care for victims of violence).

Communications media. The possibility of communications media that inform and comment upon local and global conditions from a nonkilling perspective is illustrated by work of the pioneering journalist Colman McCarthy (1994) and by several publications from around the world. They include *Day by Day,* the monthly press, arts, and sports review of Britain's pacifist Fellowship Party (London); Bangkok's Buddhist *Seeds of Peace*; the international *Peace News: for Nonviolent Revolution* (London); the French monthly *Non-violence Actualité* (Montargis); Italy's *Azione Nonviolenta* (Verona); Germany's *Graswürtzelrevolution* (Oldenburg); and the American magazines *Fellowship* (Nyack, N.Y.) and *Nonviolent Activist* (New York); among many others. Journals such as *Social Alternatives* (Brisbane, Australia), *Gandhi Marg* (New Delhi), and the *International Journal of Nonviolence* (Washington, D.C.) evoke and communicate nonviolent intellect on various social issues. Some publishing houses such as Navajivan (Ahmedabad, India), New Society Publishers (Blaine, Washington), Non-violence Actualité (Montargis, France), and Orbis Books (Maryknoll, New York) specialize in books to educate for nonviolent social change.

Cultural resources. Nonviolent cultural resources are creations of art and intellect that uplift the human spirit and inspire advances toward realization of a nonkilling society. These include folk songs ("We Shall Overcome"), opera (Philip Glass, "Satyagraha"), novels (Bertha von Suttner, *Lay Down Your Arms*); poetry (Steve Mason, *Johnny's Song*), art (Käthe Kollwitz, *Seed for the planting must not be ground*); and films (Richard Attenborough, *Gandhi*). The Centre for Nonviolence through the Arts, founded in 1995 by Mallika Sarabhai in Ahmedabad, India, seeks to synergize nonkilling creativity for social transformation in the visual, performing, and literary arts.

Nonviolent political struggles. Although not new to history, nonviolent political struggles in the last half of the twentieth century increasingly manifest nonkilling human potential. "As recent as 1980," Gene Sharp observes, "it was to most people unthinkable that nonviolent struggle—or people's power—would within a decade be recognized as a major force shaping the course of politics throughout the world" (Sharp 1989: 4). From 1970 to 1989 Sharp notes significant nonviolent struggles in at least the following places: *Africa* (Algeria, Morocco, South Africa, and Sudan), *Asia* (Burma, China, India, Japan, South Korea, Pakistan, the Philippines, and Tibet), the *Americas* (Argentina, Bolivia, Brazil, Chile, Haiti, Mexico, Nicaragua, Panama, and the United States), *Europe* (Estonia, France, East and West Germany, Hungary, Ireland, Latvia, and Yugoslavia), the *Middle East* (Israel occupied Palestine), and the *Pacific* (Australia and New Caledonia). Since 1989 demonstrations of nonviolent people's power have contributed to the dramatic end of single-party Communist rule in the former Soviet Union, Eastern Europe, the Baltic Republics, and Mongolia; to the peaceful reunification of Germany; and to the end of apartheid rule in South Africa.

Although not all nonviolent struggles have been completely violence-free, although some have been brutally repressed as in Burma in 1988 and China in 1989, and although some commentators would attribute successes to threatened lethality—they depart markedly from the bloody traditions of the American, French, Russian, Chinese, and other violent revolutions. Learning from the examples of the Gandhian independence movement in India that contributed to the collapse of the world colonial system, the Kingian movement for racial civil rights in the United States, the nonviolent people's power movement for democracy in the Philippines, the anti-nuclear war movement, environmental defense actions, and other experiences—gradually a repertoire of powerful nonviolent strategy and tactics is arising out of practice, including use of high technologies. In turn some ruling regimes are beginning to show more nonlethal restraint in countering nonviolent citizen demands for peace, freedom, and justice.

In addition to broad struggles that have shown capacities to influence regime and structural changes, many social movements have sought specific changes to establish features of a nonkilling society. Among them are movements to abolish the death penalty; for alternatives to abortion; to recognize conscientious objection to military service; to abolish armies; to establish nonviolent civilian defense; to seek nonviolent security in areas of urban and rural combat; to end war taxes; to abolish nuclear, biological, and chemical weapons; to abolish land mines, automatic weapons, and handguns; to remove economic support for lethality; to protect the human rights of individuals, minorities, and indigenous peoples; to protect the environment from despoilation; and to realize other political, military, economic, social, and cultural changes.

Advancing beyond historical spontaneity, nonviolent struggles at the end of the twentieth century—aided by the pioneering research of Gene Sharp (1973), Johan Galtung (1992; 1996), Jacques Semelin (1993), Michael Randle (1994), and others—are becoming more self-consciously principled, more creative, and more widespread through diffusion by global communications. Amidst continuing bloodshed in the era of globalization, nonviolent movements increasingly arise and diffuse throughout the world through processes of innovation and emulation to challenge the violence and injustices of state and society (Powers and Vogele 1997; Zunes, Kurtz, and Asher 1999; Ackerman and DuVall 2000).

Historical roots

History provides salient outcroppings of nonkilling capabilities, often in periods of great violence. When nonkilling manifestations are aggregated globally, a nonkilling history of humankind can be created. Some glimpses of constituent elements can now be seen.

Nonkilling conviction and commitment are irrepressible. Over two thousand years of Judaeo-Christian history, as long as the Sixth Commandment "Thou shalt not kill" (Exod. 20: 13), the Sermon on the Mount (Matt. 5–7), and the example of Christ on the Cross endure in oral or written tradition, the nonkilling imperative will continue to be reignited in courageous resistance to lethality—despite persecution and martyrdom—by some humans from illiterate peasants to privileged elites (Brock 1968; 1970; 1972; 1990; 1991a; 1991b; 1992). Such was the coordinated mass "burning of weapons" on June 29, 1895 by 7,000 pacifist Doukhobor peasants at three sites in Russia, followed by persecution and emigration of 7,500 Doukhobors to Canada in 1899, assisted by Tolstoy (Tarasoff 1995: 8–9). Historical roots of nonkilling capability can be found in other cultural traditions; for example, in Buddhism (Horigan 1996; Paige and Gilliatt 1991); Islam (Banerjee 2000; Crow 1990; Easwaran 1999; Kishtainy 1990; Paige, Satha-Anand, and Gilliatt 1993a; Satha-Anand 1990; Tayyebulla 1959); and Judaism (Schwarzschild, n.d.; Polner and Goodman 1994; Wilcock 1994).

Furthermore, as Moskos and Chambers (1993) have shown in a comparative historical study of conscientious objection to military service in modern democracies, nonsectarian, humanitarian, and political grounds for refusal to kill in war are becoming predominant. A process of secularization of nonkilling is underway. The spiritual and the secular, the principled and pragmatic, are converging in refusal to kill

Another historical observation is the surprising responsiveness of some otherwise violence-accepting political leaders to sincere and often death-defying expressions of nonkilling conviction. Among examples is the decision of King Frederick I of Prussia in 1713 to exempt pacifist Mennonites from conscription. Similar exemptions were granted to Mennonites in Russia by Catherine II (1763) and Alexander II (1875), (Brock 1972:

230, 234, 436). In 1919, Lenin, on plea of Tolstoy's companion V.G. Chertkov, and advice from Bolshevik V.C. Bonch-Bruevich, exempted Tolstoyans and other pacifist religious communities from service in the Red Army (Josephson 1985: 162; Coppieters and Zverev 1995). One of the first Bolshevik decisions was to abolish the death penalty in the army. The ephemerality of such decisions does not detract from their reality as opportunities for significant nonkilling discovery. For as Jerome D. Frank has observed, given citizen propensities to follow authority, changing the behavior of political leaders may be one of the most effective contributions that can be made to peace. But while leaders may lead, followers may lag. Zimring and Hawkins point out in a study of the abolition of the death penalty in Western democracies:

> The end of capital punishment nearly always occurs in democracies in the face of majority public opposition. Every Western democracy except the United States has ended executions, but we are aware of no nation where a democratic consensus supporting abolition was present when executions stopped. Yet abolition persists, even though public resentment remains for long periods (1986: xvi).

However, to note the importance of political leadership (Paige 1977; Burns 1978) for nonkilling social change is not to overlook the increasing force of mass nonviolent people's power.

A third historical observation is that commitment to nonkilling is characteristically accompanied by efforts to alleviate other forms of suffering and to bring about life-respecting changes in society. Nonkilling means neither unconcern nor inaction. Jain *ahimsa*, for example, extends to efforts to rescue animals, birds, and other forms of life (Tobias 1991). Nonkilling engagement in efforts to realize significant structural changes can be seen in the Gandhian movement in India. It sought not only political independence but significant economic, social, and cultural changes affecting the poor, women, minorities, caste, and inter-communal relationships. Likewise the nonviolent Kingian movement in the United States in its quest for freedom and racial equality became engaged in efforts to remove obstacles to justice in the structure and functioning of American society from poverty to war.

Evidence for nonkilling capability can be seen in the histories of even violent modern nation states. The United States of America provides an example. As yet incompletely articulated in comparison with the predominant violent tradition, the roots of nonkilling in the American experience understandably are largely unknown to students of political science. Yet pioneering inquiries reveal their unmistakable presence (Brock 1968; Cooney and Michalowski 1987; Hawkley and Juhnke 1993; Kapur 1992; Kohn 1987; Lynd and Lynd 1995; Association of American Historians 1994; Schlissel 1968; True 1995; Zinn 1990).

Nonkilling in the United States. Nonkilling was present at the creation of the United States of America. It began in peaceful relations between indigenous peoples and pacifist immigrants. For much of seventy years (1682–1756) pacifist Quakers in the militia-free colony of Pennsylvania coexisted peacefully with Delaware Indians following treaty pledges to keep doors open to friendly visits and to consult upon rumors of hostile intent (Brock 1990: 87–91). Provisions for religious conscientious objection to killing in military service were contained in the laws of twelve of thirteen pre-Revolutionary colonies. The most liberal, Rhode Island (1673), exempted men whose convictions forbade them "to train, arm, rally to fight, to kill" and provided that objectors should not "suffer any punishment, fine, distraint, penalty nor imprisonment" (Kohn 1987: 8).

Nonkilling was present in the legislative deliberations of the emerging nation. One of the first statutes passed by the Continental Congress in 1775 pledged "no violence" to nonkilling religious conscience (Kohn 1987: 10, 13). In the deliberations that added the Bill of Rights to the U.S. Constitution in 1789, Representative James Madison proposed a provision in Article 2 that would have recognized the right of every citizen to refuse to kill: "No person religiously scrupulous of bearing arms shall be compelled to render military service in person" (Kohn 1987: 11). Madison's proposal was approved by the House of Representatives, but it was rejected by a states-rights defensive Senate conference committee that objected to extending federal controls over state militias.

In the American Revolution (1775–83), colonists of various ethnicities and religious persuasions refused to kill on either side. A Bible-reading British trooper, Thomas Watson, renounced killing and later became a Massachusetts Quaker elder (Brock 1968: 280–81). During the British blockade and subsequent American siege of Boston (1774–76), pacifist Quakers persuaded contending generals Washington and Howe to allow them to deliver humanitarian aid to its citizens and refugees (Brock 1968: 193-94). Not without suffering, nonkilling conscience was assisted and respected.

It was not unthinkable that nonviolent struggle could have gained Independence (Conser, et al. 1986). According to Charles K. Whipple in *Evils of the Revolutionary War* (1839): "We should have attained independence as effectually, as speedily, as honorably, and under very much more favorable conditions, if we had not resorted to arms." The method would have been: "1st, A steady and quiet refusal to comply with unjust requisitions; 2nd, public declarations of their grievances, and demands for redress; and 3rd, patient endurance of whatever violence was used to compel their submission"(2). Whipple's analysis of the dynamics of nonviolent struggle anticipated virtually every key element in the later thought of Gandhi and Gene Sharp (1973). In calculating the advantages of nonviolent revolution, Whipple estimated that fewer lives would have been lost (perhaps 1,000 leaders and 10,000 men, women, and children versus 100,000 who died in eight years of armed struggle); the economic costs of war (135 million dollars) and subsequent militarization (300 million dollars) would have been avoided; and the spiritual and ethical foundation of the new nation would have been established at a much higher level. Furthermore, nonviolent American revolutionaries would not have continued the institution of slavery, "would not have proceeded to defraud, corrupt, and exterminate the original inhabitants of this country," and "would not have admitted the system of violence and retaliation as a constituent part of their own government," including the death penalty (10).

Nonkilling was present preceding the Civil War. Patriots, accepting suffering and sacrifice, worked for peace in wars against England (1812) and Mexico (1845), for women's rights, and especially to abolish slavery. Among them were women and men, black and white, religious and secular (Cooney and Michalowski 1987: 20–33; Lynd and Lynd 1995: 13-41). Nonviolent abolitionist efforts succeeded in passage of emancipation laws in northern legislatures. In border and southern states, some slave owners were persuaded on spiritual or economic grounds to free their slaves, continuing prophetic liberation labors of Quaker John Woolman (1720–72). Nonkilling emancipation was not unthinkable. Since the British abolished slavery at home in 1777, the slave trade in 1807, and slaveholding throughout the British Empire in 1833, slavery might have been abolished peacefully in the United States if it like Canada had maintained some form of association with the mother country.

During the Civil War (1861–65), following abuse of war resisters including torture, imprisonment, execution, and assassination, provisions for conscientious objection to killing were included in the draft laws of the Confederacy (1862) and the Union (1864). Although the laws were inconsistently applied at sometimes vindictive lower levels, appeals for exemption in individual cases were sympathetically received by Union President Abraham Lincoln, Secretary of War Edwin Stanton, and Confederate Assistant Secretary of War John A. Campbell (Moskos and Chambers 1993: 30–1). Caught in the shifting tides of war the nonkilling Tennessee Disciples of Christ first successfully petitioned Confederate President Jefferson Davis and then occupying Union military governor Andrew Johnson to exempt them from conscription (Brock 1968: 842–3). Amidst fratricidal bloodshed of civil war, nonkilling conscience was asserted and accepted to varying degrees by both sides.

Nonkilling persisted in the era of industrialization and imperialist expansion, into and beyond the three world wars of the twentieth century. Although not unmarred by employer, police, state, and sometimes worker violence, the struggle for rights to organize and improve conditions of American labor was essentially nonviolent. It was not an armed working class revolution. Nonviolent also was the movement for women's equal rights that saw election of the first woman to Congress in 1916, Representative Jeannette Rankin, Republican of Montana (Josephson 1974). In 1917 along with 49 male colleagues[8] and six Senators[9] she voted against United States entry into World War I. Reelected in 1940, she stood alone in 1941 to vote against United States engagement in World War II. Later at age 88 she led 5,000 women of the Jeannette Rankin Brigade in a march on Washington to end American killing in the Vietnam War.

In World War I, some 4,000 conscripted American men refused to kill. Thirteen hundred accepted noncombatant military duties, mainly medical; another 1,500 were assigned to agricultural labor; 940 were kept in segregated military training units; and 450 "absolutists" refusing to cooperate with killing in any way were court-martialed and confined in military prisons where seventeen died from harsh treatment and disease (Moskos and Chambers 1993: 34-5; Kohn 1987: 42; Lynd and Lynd 1995: 91–117; Schlissel 1968: 128–175).

In the period of World War II military conscription (1940–47), 72,354 men claimed conscientious objection to killing:

25,000 served in noncombatant roles; 11,996 men from 213 religious denominations agreed to work in 151 Civilian Public Service Camps (Appendix D); and 6,086 men who refused all forms of war-fighting cooperation were imprisoned. Three-fourths of the imprisoned were Jehovah's Witnesses (Anderson 1994: 1–2; Moskos and Chambers 1993: 37–8; Cooney and Michalowski 1987: 94–5; Gara and Gara 1999).

Nonkilling potential in American society appeared again during the nuclear age "Cold War" (1945–91) that in killed and wounded brought after World War II, the Civil War, and World War I the fourth and fifth most bloody wars in American history—in Vietnam (1964–75) and Korea (1950–53). In the Cold War struggle between the United States, the Soviet Union, and their allies, at least 20 million global dead were sacrificed to revolutionary, counterrevolutionary, and geopolitical state lethality. In the Korea War, some 22,500 American conscripts refused to kill. Massive resistance to the Vietnam War saw unprecedented numbers of men refusing to kill on increasingly majority secular grounds (Moskos and Chambers 1993: 39–43). In 1972 more draft registrants were classified as conscientious objectors than were conscripted. Other Vietnam war resisters evaded registration, went to jail, or escaped into exile, reversing the historic flow of pacifist immigrants to the United States who had sought freedom from conscription in their homelands. Amidst the slaughter in Vietnam, unarmed conscientious objectors to killing who had agreed to serve in noncombatant roles such as front-line medical corpsmen became confirmed in rejection of war (Gioglio 1989).

In the twilight of the Cold War, nonkilling conviction rose to salience once again in the Persian Gulf War against Iraq (1991). This time it was not a case of civilians resisting induction since no conscription was in effect, but of serving members of the armed forces and reserves who refused to kill. Fifty Marines claiming conscientious objection were court-martialed and imprisoned (Moskos and Chambers 1993: 44).

Nonkilling potential in American history is evident in efforts to abolish the death penalty. Beginning in colonial times with reduction in the number of crimes demanding death, through abolition except for treason by the territory of Michigan (1846), and complete abolition by Rhode Island (1852) and Wisconsin (1853), currently twelve of fifty states plus the District of Columbia demonstrate that Americans collectively in civil life as well as individually in war can refuse to kill. At the federal level, however, the Supreme Court has yet to rule decisively that execution of citizens violates the U.S. Constitution (Zimring and Hawkins 1986).

Among other roots of nonkilling potential in the United States are struggles for a nuclear weapon-free society (Swords into Plowshares movement), for a society without the militarized violence of poverty (Catholic Worker movement), for an end to the male-dominated culture of violence against women (women's movement), and for recognition of the equality of African-Americans and all races in a free and just society (Kingian movement for nonviolent social change). Meeting with African-American leaders in 1936, Gandhi was told that his message of nonviolence resonated strongly with "Negro spirituals" and that African-Americans were ready to receive it. Gandhi replied, "It may be through the Negroes that the unadulterated message of nonviolence will be delivered to the world" (Kapur 1992: 89–90). Thus in interactions between the Gandhian, Kingian, and other world nonviolent movements—as in its indigenous and immigrant pacifist roots—nonviolence in America is inextricably linked to the nonkilling history of the world.

Despite its dominant violence-celebrating political tradition, roots of a nonkilling American society can be seen in irrepressible reassertion of the life-respecting ethic from the colonial era to the present. They are evident in refusal to kill in war; in opposition to the death penalty; in objection to abortion; in demands for disarmament; in resistance to militarization and violent global power projection; in nonviolent actions for structural change in economics, race relations, women's rights, and cultural identity; and in religious, artistic, and literary expressions (True 1995). The historical elements are observable for what can become nonviolent patriotism or "nonviolent nationalism," as Gwynfor Evans, a founder of the Welsh pacifist political party Plaid Cymru, has eloquently argued for Wales (Evans 1972). Its anthem could be "America the Beautiful," its marching song "We Shall Overcome," and its prayer "God bless nonviolent America and nonviolence in the world."

Nonkilling Lives. Ultimately the roots of a nonkilling society lie in the biography of humankind. Men and women, singly and in concert, celebrated and unsung, past and present, demonstrate potential for combining commitment not to kill with positive pursuit of social change. What some can do, others can do also.

At the entrance to the Musée d'Art Moderne de la Ville de Paris there is a great circular mural by Raoul Dufy that depicts contributors to the discovery and use of electricity from ancient philosophers to modern scientists and inventors. Analogously one can envision a vast panorama of global contributors to the spirit, theory, and practice of nonviolence welcoming scholars who enter study of nonkilling political science. A glimpse of the global heritage can be seen in the Biographical Dictionary of Modern Peace Leaders (Josephson 1985) that records the lives of 717 persons in thirty-nine countries who lived from 1800 to 1980. Read from cover to cover its 1,134 pages offer a liberal arts education in vocations and methods for seeking a nonviolent world. Values range from temporary acceptance of violence to complete commitment to nonkilling principles. Extension of such inquiry historically, geographically, culturally, and in contemporary life, will reveal and inspire a global legacy of nonkilling courage and commitment. Universal discovery and sharing of nonkilling lives is needed.

Nonkilling lives interact and resonate across time, cultures, and space. Ancient rulers set examples: In Egypt, the Nubia-born pharaoh Shabaka (c.760–c.695 B.C.E.) abolishes the death penalty (Bennett 1988: 11). In India, Buddhist emperor Ashoka renounces war and killing of living beings following the conquest of Kalinga (c. 262 B.C.E.) that left 100,000 dead, 150,000 in exile, and countless deaths and suffering of the innocent (Chowdhury 1997: 52). Nonkilling examples of spiritual leaders evoke creative emulation across generations: the Buddha, Mahavira, Jesus, Muhammad, George Fox, Guru Nanak, Bahá'u'lláh, and others. Dramatic changes, secular and spiritual, occur as individuals shift from killing to nonkilling. Soldiers become pacifists (Crozier 1938; Tendulkar 1967; Khan 1997; Boubalt, Gauchard, and Muller 1986; Roussel 1997). Revolutionaries renounce lethality (Narayan 1975; Bendaña 1998). Conscientious objectors resist military conscription (Moskos and Chambers 1993).On humanist grounds, New Zealand's Archibald Baxter resists torture and World War I battlefield conscription with incredible nonkilling bravery (Baxter 2000). A Bible-reading Austrian peasant, Franz Jägerstätter, is beheaded for refusing to fight for Hitler (Zahn 1964). Nonviolent rescuers risk their lives to save Jews from Hitler's Holocaust (Fogelman 1994; Hallie 1979). Individuals withdraw moral, material, and labor support for the war-fighting, modern military-industrial state (Everett 1989). Others seek directly to disable weapons of mass destruction (Norman 1989; Polner and O'Grady 1997).

Anonymous millions respond to the nonviolent leadership of a small, five-foot four-inch Indian, Mohandas K. Gandhi. Culturally violent Pathans respond to the nonviolent Muslim leadership of Abdul Ghaffar Khan (Banerjee 2000; Easwaran 1999). As the great Gandhian educator Dr. G. Ramachandran has observed, "The unknown heroes and heroines of nonviolence are more important than those that are known" (Ramachandran 1983). In the United States a small group of African-American college students, trained in Gandhian methods, initiate the civil rights movement that thrusts into leadership the Reverend Dr. Martin Luther King, Jr. (Halberstam 1998). Nonviolent Americans, such as Adin Ballou and Henry David Thoreau inspire Tolstoy (Christian 1978: 588); Tolstoy inspires Gandhi; Gandhi inspires King; all inspire German Green Party founder Petra Kelly (Kelly 1989) and many others in a cumulative global diffusion process of emulation and innovation. In 1997 and 1998 Gandhi was chosen as most admired world leader by more than two hundred young leaders from over sixty countries participating in the first two training programs of the United Nations University's International Leadership Academy held in Amman, Jordan. Their admiration echoes that of many independence movement leaders in the post-1945 breakdown of the world colonial system.

Nonviolent leaders continue to arise throughout the world: among them Maha Ghosananda of Cambodia, Ham Suk Hon of Korea, Ken Saro-Wiwa of Nigeria, A.T. Ariyaratne of Sri Lanka, Sulak Sivaraksa of Thailand, Lanzo del Vasto and General Jacques de Bollardière of France, Ronald Mallone of England, Aldo Capitini of Italy, N. Radhakrishan of India, Dom Helder Camara of Brazil, A.J. Muste of the United States. Reversing historical neglect of Gandhi, Nobel peace prizes begin to recognize leaders with salient commitments to nonviolence: Albert J. Luthuli and Desmond Tutu of South Africa, Mairead Corrigan Maguire of Northern Ireland, Adolfo Perèz Esquivel of Argentina, Aung San Suu Kyi of Burma, the Dalai Lama of Tibet.

Women—each with her story—courageously step forward to challenge nonviolently conditions of violence in every aspect of society: Bertha von Suttner of Austria; Gedong Bagoes Oka of Bali; Medha Patkar of India; Dorothy Day, Barbara Deming, and Jean Toomer (Stanfield 1993: 49) of the United States. In World War II Britain 1,704 women claim conscientious objection to conscription and 214 who refuse to support war through noncombatant or civilian service are imprisoned

(Harries-Jenkins 1993: 77). Collectively women take powerful stands against militarist human rights atrocities (Mothers of the Plaza de Mayo, Buenos Aires), ethnic slaughter (Women in Black, Serbia), preparation for nuclear war (Greenham Common Women's Peace Camp, Britain), ecological destruction (Chipko hug-the-trees movement, India), and many other injustices (McAllister 1982, 1988; Morgan 1984; Foster 1989). Scholars such as Joan V. Bondurant (1969), Elise Boulding (1980; 1992), and Berenice A. Carroll (1998) advance knowledge for nonviolent social change.

Collegial gender pairs, married or not, provide mutual support in nonviolent transformational struggles: Kasturba and Mohandas Gandhi, Coretta Scott and Martin Luther King, Jr., Dolores Huerta and Cesar Chavez, Dorothy Day and Peter Maurin, Frances May Witherspoon and Charles Recht, Elizabeth McAllister and Philip Berrigan. Co-gender people's power is writ large in the nonviolent Philippine democratic intervention of 1986, when nuns, priests, laywomen, and laymen combined to confront dictatorship and the threat of counterrevolutionary military bloodshed (Santiago, A.S. 1995). Viewed globally, the nonviolent biography of humankind inspires confidence that men and women are capable of creating killing-free, just societies that respect the needs of all.

Capabilities for a Nonkilling Society

The possibility of a nonkilling society is rooted in human experience and creative capabilities. The vast majority of human beings have not killed and do not kill. Although we are capable of killing, we are not by nature compelled to kill. However imperfectly followed, the main teaching of the great spiritual traditions is: respect life, do not kill. To this teaching, humans, under the most violent circumstances, have shown themselves capable of responding in brain and being with complete devotion. Where killing does occur, scientific creativity promises unprecedented ability to understand its causes, how to remove them, and how to assist liberation of self and society from lethality.

Prototypical components of a nonkilling society already exist in past and present global experience. They are not the product of hypothetical imagination. Spiritual, political, economic, social, and cultural institutions and practices based upon nonkilling principles can be found in human experience. There are army-free, execution-free, and virtually weapon-free societies. There are nonkilling organizations and movements dedicated to solving problems that threaten the survival and well-being of humankind. Nonkilling historical experience provides knowledge to inform present and future transformative action. There is a great legacy of nonkilling lives, past and present, individuals whose courage and works inspire and instruct.

If any people decided to combine, adapt, and creatively add to the components that already exist in global human experience, a reasonable approximation of a nonkilling society is even now within reach. To assert possibility, of course, is not to guarantee certainty but to make problematical the previously unthinkable and to strengthen confidence that we humans are capable of nonkilling global transformation.

Chapter 3

IMPLICATIONS FOR POLITICAL SCIENCE

> Nonviolence is not only a matter of religion.
> Nonviolence is not only a matter of society.
> Nonviolence is the science of power.
>
> G. Ramachandran

What are the implications of capabilities for realizing nonkilling societies for the academic discipline of political science? If the premise of nonkilling potentiality replaced the assumption of lethal inescapability, what kind of science would political scientists seek to create? What values would inspire and guide our work? What facts would we seek? What explanatory and predictive theories would we explore? What uses of knowledge would we facilitate? How would we educate and train ourselves and others? What institutions would we build? And how would we engage with others in processes of discovery, creation, sharing, and use of knowledge to realize nonkilling societies for a nonkilling world?

The assumed attainability of a nonkilling society implies a disciplinary shift to nonkilling creativity. It calls into question the Weberian dogma that acceptance of violence (killing) is imperative for the practice and science of politics, and that the ethic of nonkilling is incompatible with them. It makes the previously unthinkable at the very least problematical.

Logic of Nonkilling Political Analysis

A nonkilling political science paradigm shift implies need for a four-part logic of nonkilling political analysis. We need to know the causes of killing; the causes of nonkilling; the causes of transition between killing and nonkilling; and the characteristics of completely killing-free societies.

Paradoxically the need to understand killing is more acute for nonkilling political science than for the conventional violence-assuming discipline. This salience derives from the goal of contributing by nonkilling means to conditions where lethality and its correlates are absent. Where killing is assumed to be inevitable and acceptable for personal and collective purposes, there is less urgency to understand and to remove the causes of lethality—one's own, that of others, and these in interaction. There is a sense of security, albeit problematic, in the assumption that in the last analysis "I/we will kill you." Where this assumption is absent, to understand and to remove the causes of killing are absolutely essential for survival and well-being.

The concept of causation is central to nonkilling analysis. Wherever killing occurs—from homicide to genocide to atomic annihilation—we need to understand processes of cause and effect, however complex and interdependent. Every case of killing demands causal explanation. We need to know who kills whom, how, where, when, why and with what antecedents, contextual conditions, individual and social meanings, and consequences. And, of course, we need to discover cross-case patterns of lethal causality for intensive, parsimonious, typological explanation.

Similarly we need to understand the causes of nonkilling. Why do humans not kill? Why has the idea of nonkilling arisen in human life? Why have humans committed themselves to nonkilling principles? Why have some people throughout history—in the face of ridicule, ostracism, exile, deprivation, imprisonment, torture, mutilation, and threats of death up to assassination, execution, and collective extermination—held fast to the principle of life over lethality? Why have they created policies, practices, and institutions to achieve nonkilling ends by nonkilling means?

Furthermore what are the causes of transition, individually and collectively, from killing to nonkilling—and from nonkilling to killing? Why have killers shifted from acceptance to rejection of taking human life? Why have soldiers become pacifists, revolutionaries renounced lethality, and murderers become committed to nonkilling? Why have ideas, individuals, leaders, organizations, institutions, and policies shifted to nonviolence? And why have persons previously committed to nonkilling shifted to participate in and support bloodshed—as when some states abolish and reimpose death penalties and some pacifists temporarily support specific wars? Nonkilling analysis does not assume irreversible linear progression. Understanding of the incidence, magnitude, and causes of oscillation in transition to nonkilling conditions is essential for facilitation of nonkilling change. Attention is directed from individuals through structural components to whole societies.

A fourth requirement for nonkilling political analysis is to understand the characteristics of completely killing-free societies under the assumption of hypothetically infinite variation among them. Given human inventiveness, there is no assumption of necessary homogeneity. This fourth requirement presents arguably the most creative task, although all call for utmost creativity. The first three require validation of findings derived from historical or contemporary contexts. The fourth combines knowledge from them in progressive explorations of ethically acceptable, potentially achievable, and sometimes hypothetically envisioned conditions of individual, social, and global life. This challenges us as does the poet Walt Whitman, "To leap beyond, yet nearer bring" (Whitman 1977(1855): 71).

It is assumed that no society, hitherto restrained by killing-prone characteristics, has yet demonstrated the full range of nonkilling qualities of which humans are capable. But by drawing upon historical and contemporary experiences on a global scale—and by hypothetically combining demonstrated capabilities—new nonkilling possibilities for any society can be apprehended. Furthermore, such empirically-grounded insights need to be extended in explorations of "pure theory" to identify desirable characteristics of killing-free societies and plausible processes of realizing them from present conditions.

Hitherto, unlike sciences that encourage development of pure theory as a contribution to practical applications (such as in mathematics, physics, and economics), political science has tended to be unreceptive to hypothetical theoretical imagination. This is especially true where violence is concerned. Violence-assuming political science tends to discourage nonviolent creativity. By dismissing it in professional training as deviantly "utopian," "idealistic," and "unrealistic," political science intellect is condemned to confinement in perpetual lethality. Nonkilling creativity offers promise of liberation.

Basic knowledge from nonkilling analysis needs to be applied in transformational action to create alternatives in five zones of what can be portrayed as a funnel of killing.

Figure 1

FUNNEL OF KILLING.

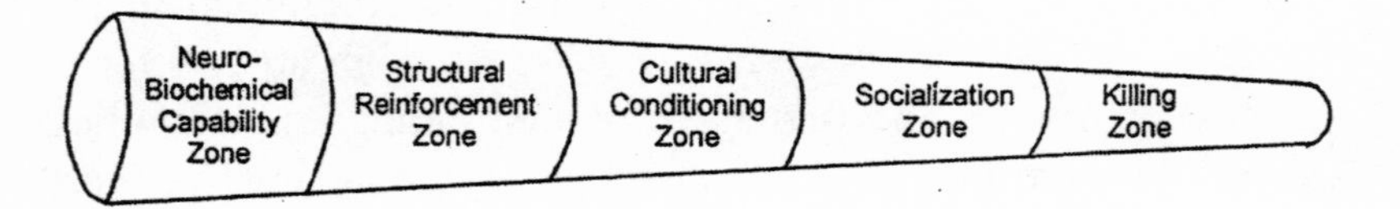

The *killing zone* is the place of bloodshed from homicide to mass annihilation. The *socialization zone* is where people learn to kill, directly by training or vicariously by observation of models for emulation. In the *cultural conditioning zone* we are predisposed to accept killing as unavoidable and legitimate. Among sources of conditioning are religions, political "isms," celebrations of triumphs and atrocities, family traditions, law, mass communications, and the arts. The *structural reinforcement zone* provides the socioeconomic relationships, institutions, and material means that predispose to and support killing. The *neuro-biochemical capability zone* comprises physical, neurological, and brain function factors and processes that contribute to human capacity for predatory or survival-seeking lethality and for nonkilling behavior (Lopez-Reyes 1998; Morton 2000).

The task of nonkilling transformation can be envisioned as changing the funnel of killing into an unfolding fan of nonkilling alternatives by purposive efforts within and across each zone (Figure 2). Such changes can range from spiritual and nonlethal high technology interventions in the killing zone, through nonkilling socialization and cultural conditioning, to restructuring socioeconomic conditions so that they neither produce nor require lethality for maintenance or change, and to clinical, pharmacological, physical, and self-transformative meditative and biofeedback interventions that liberate from bio-propensity to kill.

Figure 2

UNFOLDING FAN OF NONKILLING ALTERNATIVES.

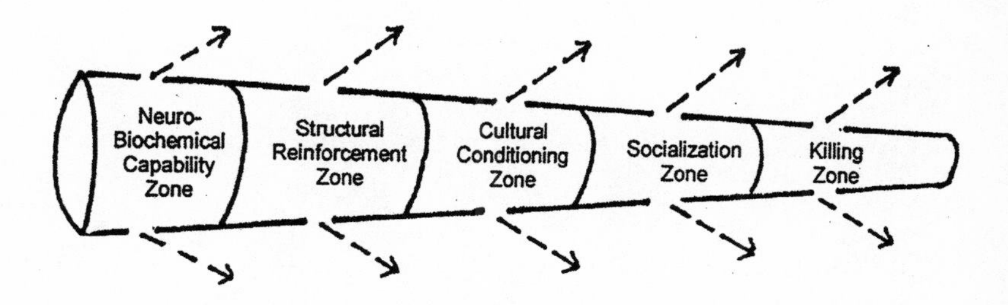

Nonkilling Action Principles

In addition to seeking knowledge required by the logic of nonviolent political analysis as related to the tasks of creating nonviolent alternatives in zones that converge on killing, a nonkilling paradigm shift requires perfection of principles to assist individual and social decisions from daily life to global politics. These can be advanced by an experimental validation approach that combines practical experience and exploratory simulations. Military human-computer and "virtual reality" combat simulations of this kind are already far advanced.

Among nonviolent principles that have arisen in salient twentieth century actions (as in the Gandhian and Kingian movements) that merit consideration are:

Draw strength from life-respecting inspiration, whether religious or humanist.

Respect your own life and lives of others.

Seek the well-being of all. Violence divides; nonviolence unites.

In conflict, from beginning to end seek reconciliation not humiliation, degradation, predation, or annihilation.

Join in constructive service to remove conditions of suffering of those in need.

Be creative. It has taken great creativity to reach present conditions of technological and structural violence. It will require greater creativity for nonkilling transformation.

Adopt an experimental approach to change. Seek successive approximations of nonkilling societies, learning from successes and failures.

Respect both individual and large-scale social action, from the influence of moral example to mass nonviolent people's power.

Be constructively courageous. Withdraw support from violence and commit it to strengthen nonviolent alternatives.

Walk lightly upon the earth. Reduce demands upon nature and fellow human beings that contribute to killing.

Each person who participates in processes of nonviolent discovery and action can contribute to perfecting progressively more powerful principles and skills for nonkilling affirmation of global life that are appropriate for specific situations and contexts.

In the context of contemporary political science, recognition of the possibility of realizing nonkilling societies raises questions for every aspect of our discipline. In general orientation toward the inevitability and legitimacy of violence, political scientists like other members of society find ourselves variously inclined toward the following views: *proviolent*—consider killing positively beneficial for self or civilization; *violence-prone*—inclined to kill or to support killing when advantageous; *ambiviolent*—equally inclined to kill or not to kill, and to support or oppose it; *violence-avoiding*—predisposed not to kill or to support it but prepared to do so; *nonviolent*—committed not to kill and to change conditions conducive to lethality. Taken as a whole the first four orientations can be said to characterize violence-assuming or violence-accepting politics and political science. The last orientation calls for creation of nonkilling political science, whose task is to contribute to a nonviolent shift in science and society.

In characterizing contemporary political science as predominantly "violence-accepting" in manifest or latent assumptions, this is not to imply that all political scientists exhort their students in classrooms to "Kill! Kill!" like military drill sergeants and officers. Nor is it to neglect the violence-avoiding contributions of political scientists who seek to substitute democratic institutions (such as party competitions, elections, legislatures, and law) to replace civil and international war. But recognition of the violence-accepting nature of the present discipline and the possibility of nonkilling alternatives offers promise of ethical-empirical and empirical-ethical advancement. It implies the need to place nonkilling along with questions of freedom, equality, justice, and democracy, at the normative-empirical and empirical-normative core of the discipline.

Nonviolent Scientific Revolution

Recognition of the possibility of realizing nonkilling societies implies a nonviolent scientific revolution in political science. Seven interdependent sub-revolutions are needed: a *normative revolution* from acceptance of killing to rejection; a *factual revolution* to identify factors favorable for nonkilling social transformation; a *theoretical revolution* to understand causes and processes of nonkilling change; an *educational and training revolution* to provide knowledge and skills for nonkilling transformation; an *applied revolution* to engage nonkilling knowledge in practice; an *institutional revolution* to transform and create organizations to facilitate nonkilling change; and a *methodological revolution* to create and adapt methods of inquiry, analysis, and action most suitable for nonkilling transformational tasks.

Normative revolution. The implied normative shift is from the killing imperative to the imperative not to kill. One way this can occur is by a cumulative, value-added process of interacting ethical and empirical discoveries. Ethically the implied progression is from killing is ethically imperative, to killing is questionably imperative, to nonkilling is hypothetically explorable, to nonkilling normative commitment. The parallel empirical progression is from nonkilling societies are impossible, to nonkilling societies are problematical, to actual and hypothetical exploration of characteristics of nonkilling societies, to scientific commitment to seek knowledge to create and sustain nonkilling societies in a nonkilling world.

Through such interpenetrating processes of ethical challenge and empirical response—and empirical challenge and ethical response—the impenetrable barrier posited by Weber between nonviolent principles and violent politics can be crossed. In this way uncompromising respect for life can be added to "uncompromising commitment to rules of evidence and inference" (Almond 1996: 89) as a common ethical basis for contemporary academic political science.

Figure 3

PROCESS OF NORMATIVE-EMPIRICAL NONKILLING PARADIGM SHIFT.

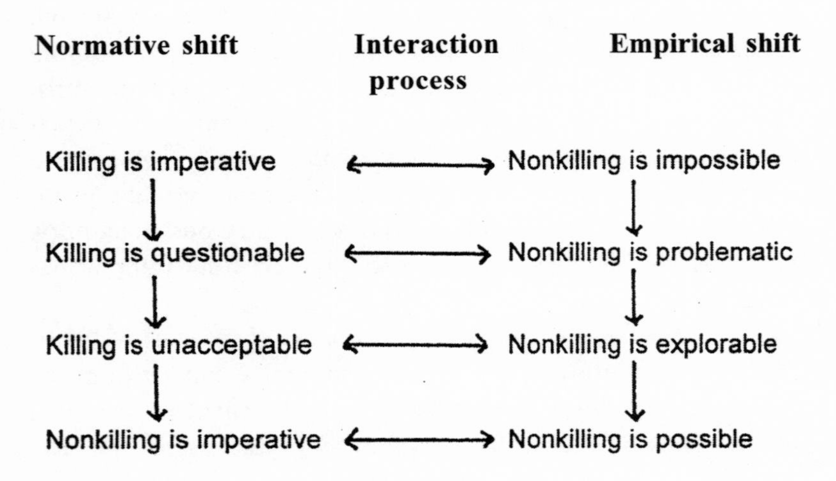

Factual revolution. Factually a nonkilling shift implies purposive recovery and discovery of evidence for nonkilling human capabilities that tend to be overlooked or deemphasized by violence-accepting assumptions. Such facts may range from neuroscience to nonlethal high technologies. Of special interest are manifestations of nonviolence in otherwise violent historical and cultural conditions. For example, in Greece in 399 B.C.E., an estimated 140 out of 500 Athenian senators voted not to condemn Socrates to death (Stone 1989: 187). In Japan, during the Buddhist Heian period (794—1192), "capital punishment was not practiced for about three hundred and fifty years" (Nakamura 1967: 145). In the United States on April 4 and 6, 1917, six Senators[8] and fifty Representatives[9] voted against declaring war on Germany. In Russia, on October 23, 1917, officially at least two and perhaps as many as five or six Bolsheviks on the Central Committee opposed adoption of Lenin's policy of armed revolution (Shub 1976: 271). In the United States, in late July 1945 on the eve of the Hiroshima and Nagasaki atomic bomb attacks, nineteen of 150 Manhattan Project scientists voted against any military use of the weapon they had helped to create (Giovannitti and Freed 1965: 168; Alperovitz 1995). In 1996 the United States Marine Corps became the "executive agent" to coordinate all Department of Defense and other governmental activities for research, development, and acquisition of nonlethal weapons (Lewer and Schofield 1997: 45). The latter constitutes a precursor of a shift to nonkilling security thinking, although such weapons presently are employed as an adjunct to lethal technologies and can still maim and kill.

A nonkilling factual shift seeks to discover past and present indicators of nonkilling propensities in every society.

Theoretical revolution. The implied theoretical revolution is to create normative and empirical theories that advance knowledge required by the logic of nonkilling analysis and that contribute to individual decisions, civil society actions, and public policies. For example, the combination of three pioneering sources of theoretical insight—*principled, pragmatic,* and *processual*—offers promise of gaining extraordinary insight into the transforming potential of nonkilling political power. The first is the conventionally overlooked Gandhian stress upon the importance of life-respecting spiritual force in truth-seeking (justice-seeking) individual and collective actions as set forth, for example, in Gandhi's *The Science of*

Satyagraha (1970). For Gandhi, a living faith in God, defined as truth, love, and nonviolence—encompassing all religions—is the unconquerable source of nonviolent power. The spirit and reality of nonviolence is the basic law of human life; violence is a violation.

The second is the theory of nonviolent power as presented in Gene Sharp's *The Politics of Nonviolent Action* (1973). Based upon penetrating analysis of the obedience-dependent nature of political power, Sharp presents a wide repertoire of historically demonstrated techniques for nonviolent struggle, and provides a strategic analysis of the dynamics of nonviolent political transformation. Sharp's thesis is that nonviolent political action is simply pragmatically powerful: no *a priori* commitments to spiritual, religious, or pacifist principles are needed.

A third source of insight to challenge nonkilling theoretical imagination is John Burton's needs-deprivation analysis of the origins of violence and prescription of needs-satisfying processes of participation for nonviolent transformation. Burton's theory is presented in *Deviance, Terrorism & War: The Process of Solving Unsolved Social and Political Problems* (1979) and other works (1984, 1996, 1997). Burton's thesis is that all forms of lethality from homicide to war derive from violation of human needs, first among which is recognition of identity and dignity. Violators and the violated have the same needs. Under conditions of violation, neither appeal to values nor coercive control can suppress lethality. But provision of processes of problem-solving in which all whose needs are violated can participate in seeking their satisfaction offers promise for realizing nonviolent societies in a nonviolent world.

These insights into spiritual force, pragmatical efficacy, and participatory problem-solving suggest elements of nonviolent theory that can be causally contextualized in terms of history, state, class, economy, institutions, gender, race, ethnicity, religion, culture, environment, future expectations, and other aspects of local and global conditions. Important contributions to contextualizing and advancing creativity in nonviolent theory are found in Robert J. Burrowes (1996), Berenice A. Carroll (1998), Johan Galtung (1996), Brian Martin (1989), and Kate McGuinness (1993).

Applied revolution. Combined normative, factual, and theoretical shifts imply new applied commitments for nonkilling political science. The normative shift implies new interest in and constructive (but not uncritical) support for nonkilling thought, individuals, organizations, movements, policies, and institutions. Sharp's theory suggests explicit commitments to assist nonviolent transformation of violently repressive regimes and may be extended to influence or change unresponsive democratic systems. Burton's theory suggests that the central applied role of political science is to assist participatory processes of social and political problem-solving that are nonviolently responsive to human needs. Gandhian theory, fusing ethics, methods, and sensitivity to need deprivations explicitly suggests commitments to assist changing conditions of political, economic, social, and cultural structural violence that are both products and producers of killing and threats to kill. It is to be recalled that leaders inspired by nonkilling spiritual principles, such as Gandhi and King, have been profoundly committed to nonviolent structural change.

Drawing upon knowledge required by the logic of nonkilling analysis, and informed by tasks of transforming the funnel of killing into a widening fan of nonviolent alternatives, the challenge of applied nonkilling political science is to assist local and global transformation. The persistence of individual and collective lethality under contemporary conditions of "democratic politics" and "free markets" suggests that as presently constituted these are problematic guarantors of human well-being. These conditions, combined in interaction with "undemocratic politics" and "unfree markets," pose challenges for applied nonkilling political science creativity.

Educational revolution. Progress toward nonkilling political science implies shifts in professional training of political scientists and in educational service to other members of society. Rather than reflecting and affirming lethal traditions and conditions, either explicitly or tacitly, political science education must become a significant contributor to nonkilling global change. The explicit goal becomes nurturance of leadership and citizenship for nonkilling societies. The challenge is to develop competencies for research, teaching, consultancy, leadership, civic action, and critical reflection—through discovery, recovery, and sharing of nonkilling knowledge.

Nonkilling political science training will require extraordinary self-knowledge among participants—akin to that expected of psychiatrists and spiritual counselors. We need to understand the origins and implications of our own beliefs, attitudes, and emotions toward violence and nonviolence. Self-understanding is prerequisite for nonviolent social change. Training in scientific methods of meditation open to diverse spiritual approaches is appropriate. Opportunities for sharing personal and professional growth experiences for mutual benefit and support need to be provided. Nonkilling political scientists should seek mutually supportive lifetime advancement, personally and collegially, in expressing profound respect for life, however diverse we may be in other matters. These needs do not differ from those of all other members of society.

In preparation for consultancy and applied roles, nonkilling political scientists need to aspire to competencies no less than those expected of medical researchers, physicians, and teachers of physicians—and in other life and death professions. The contributions of political scientists to nonkilling societies should become no less important than those of medical professionals for individual and public health. They both share life and death concern for the importance of diagnosis, prescription, and treatment based upon the best new knowledge.

At the same time, every member of society can become a contributor to nonkilling global transformation. The educational task of nonkilling political science is to offer each participant-colleague at every level opportunities for personal development, and acquisition of knowledge and skills that will assist lifetime amplification of nonviolent leadership and citizenship. All teach; all learn.

In education, curriculum design is guided by the knowledge requirements of nonkilling analysis, the need for applied skills to transform propensities to kill into nonkilling alternatives, and the need to perfect principles to guide individual and social action. An introductory course or core seminar should confront participants vividly with the most horrific evidence of historical and contemporary human capacity for lethality that can be presented. Together we then confront a lifelong challenge: the task of our discipline is to contribute to the end of human killing. A second educational experience should introduce just as vividly global evidence for nonkilling human potential. A third component introduces individual and social transformations and oscillations. The fourth core experience reviews human inventiveness in devising political institutions for desirable societies and challenges creativity in envisioning characteristics of killing-free societies and possible ways in which political science can contribute to them. Local to global knowledge and needs, as well as global-local interactions, are introduced in each component.

Upon such foundations, nonkilling educational innovations can build. An example of an undergraduate course on nonviolent political alternatives that has evoked meaningful engagement and shared creativity has been to invite each participant to choose an aspect of violence of personal concern; to review existing literature on its nature and causes; to consult local persons who deal directly with such violence for their ideas about incidence, trends, causes, and alternatives; to think creatively for themselves about alternatives; to share analyses and problem-solving proposals with each other; and to seek consensus on proposals in a group process of social decision-making.

Methodological revolution. Methodologically a nonkilling shift challenges new thinking in methods for research, education, applied politics, and institution-building. The challenge is to adapt existing methods for nonkilling discovery and application, to devise new methods as needed, and to encourage other disciplines such as neuroscience to apply their methods in solving problems of nonkilling transformation. Especially challenging is the need for methods for research and intervention in the killing zone, as well as those suitable for analysis within and across the convergent zones of lethality.

Nonkilling political science can draw upon an ever-widening repertoire of methods of inquiry that now includes at least philosophical, historical, institutional, and legal analysis; interviewing; participant observation; case studies; comparative analysis; content analysis; textual interpretation; game theory; public choice analysis; statistical inference; survey research; laboratory and field experimentation; human and computer simulation; and various combinations of these according to purpose. Educational methods range from traditional lectures, reading-viewing, and discussion through research apprenticeships and internships, to self-guided computer explorations of the world of learning. Political applications include constitutional design, conflict resolution, organizational consultancy, electoral advice, media commentary, security policy advice, and direct leader-citizen participation in processes of social decision-making. The methodological question posed to this vast array of intellect and skills is "How can old and new methods best contribute to removal of lethality from the human condition?"

Institutional revolution. Institutionally a nonkilling paradigm shift implies questions about how the discipline of political science should be organized, what its subdisciplines should be, and what should be its relationships with other disciplines and institutions of society. It implies raising questions from a nonkilling perspective within existing structures of the discipline from global, national, and local levels. It also implies the possibility of creating new nonkilling political science departments in newly founded institutions or even creating a new transdisciplinary or hybrid profession to serve nonviolent social needs.

As presently constituted the global profession of political science is represented by the International Political Science Association (IPSA), founded in 1949. Forty-two national political science associations with a total of at least 35,689 members comprise its core membership and are represented institutionally on the IPSA executive committee (Appendix A). Diverse member interests are structurally expressed in eighteen main fields, thirty-eight research committees, and twelve study groups (Appendix B). To this can be added political scientists in countries not represented by national associations and by the many students taught by world political scientists.

A New Handbook of Political Science (Goodin and Klingemann, eds., 1996), with forty-two authors grows out of an IPSA project to survey the present state of the discipline. Eight major subdisciplines are identified and reviewed in light of developments over two decades: political institutions (rational choice, legal perspectives), political behavior (reasoning voters and multiparty systems, institutional and experiential approaches), comparative politics (macro-behavioral perspectives, democratization studies), international relations (neo-realism and neo-liberalism, post-positivist and feminist perspectives), political theory (philosophical traditions, empirical theory), public policy and administration (comparative policy analysis; ideas, interests, and institutions), political economy (sociological and Downsian perspectives), and political methodology (qualitative methods, research design and experimental methods). As introduced by the IPSA president, "There could be no better volume to take political science into the new century" (xii).

Nevertheless, despite accomplishments, *A New Handbook* demonstrates the need for nonkilling disciplinary transformation. For example, in the index there are no entries for "violence" or "nonviolence" and none for "homicide," "genocide," "capital punishment," "military," "terrorism," or "police." There are sixty entries for "war" and eight for "peace." In the index of names, "Hitler" and "Lenin" are mentioned but not "Gandhi" and "King." The name and works of the world's leading political science scholar on the theory and practice of nonviolent political struggle for democracy, national defense, and prevention of military coups—Gene Sharp and *The Politics of Nonviolent Action* (1973)—are not mentioned. Nor are the name and contributions of the seminal theorist of nonviolent conflict resolution, John Burton (1979, 1984). There is scant recognition of the work of the preeminent global peace studies pioneer Johan Galtung (1996).

IPSA's largest and oldest national component with some 13,300 members is the American Political Science Association (APSA), founded in 1903. Member interests are structured in eight major fields, ninety-six subfields, and thirty-one special interest sections (see Appendix C). The APSA and IPSA interest structures are generally similar. The main fields of American political science are: American government and politics, comparative politics, international politics, methodology, political philosophy and theory, public law and courts, public policy, and public administration. Although there are special sections on "conflict processes," and "international security and arms control" no institutional structures focus explicitly upon the knowledge and problem-solving requirements of the logic of nonkilling political analysis and action. There are for example no special sections on "violence," "nonviolence," or even "peace" (compare the International Peace Research Association). It appears that the cultural assumption that lethally-rooted and defended democracy is the best hope for the advancement of civilization has inhibited explicit institutional focus upon exploration of nonkilling civilizational alternatives.

A nonkilling shift implies raising questions within and across existing fields and subfields within the discipline as represented in the topic structure of the American and international political science associations. "What can you tell us about possibilities of nonkilling societies and nonkilling means of realizing them?" This means both to draw upon existing accomplishments and to introduce new elements. For example, this can be illustrated by raising questions within the four "traditional" fields of American political science that underlie contemporary proliferating diversity: political philosophy and theory, American government and politics, comparative politics, and international relations.

Political Philosophy and Theory

In political philosophy and theory, a nonkilling shift means to review the heritage of political thought in every culture to recover nonviolent insights and to introduce new nonkilling creativity. In Plato's *Republic,* for example, Dennis Dalton finds the ethical ideal of "non-injury" to which philosophers and political leadership should aspire, despite Plato's acceptance of war, capital punishment, and a military culture. This ideal is reflected in Plutarch's observation, "For a resort to the knife is not the mark of either a good physician or statesman, but in both cases shows a lack of skill, and in the case of the statesman, there is added both injustice and cruelty" (Plutarch 10: 249). In the Chinese tradition, compare the observation of Mencius (c.371–c.289 B.C.E.): "He who, using force, makes a pretence at virtue is a Pa (tyrant). . . . He who, using virtue, practices human heartedness (jen) is a King (wang)" (Fung 1952: 112). Also in the Chinese tradition, the thought of Mo

Tzu (Mo Ti, c.468–c.376 B.C.E.), Chinese critic of war and oppression, and philosopher of "universal love" invites global rediscovery (Fung 1952: 76–105).

Classical texts supportive of violence can be reinterpreted to subtract lethality but to retain and advance nonviolent insights. Examples can be found in Chaiwat Satha-Anand's reinterpretation of Machiavelli in *The Nonviolent Prince* (1981) and in Burrowes's reinterpretation of Clausewitz's *On War* to derive principles for nonviolent strategic defense (1996). Both are reminiscent of Gandhi's derivation of principles for nonviolent action from Lord Krishna's advice to the warrior hero Arjuna in the Hindu spiritual classic *Bhagavad Gita* (Gandhi 1971).

The violence-accepting classics of the past challenge present and future nonviolent creativity. If Plato can propose a republic governed by rulers expressing military virtues, now a nonviolent republic can be envisioned with courageous leaders and citizens committed to nonkilling principles. If Aristotle can describe constitutions for war-fighting polities, we can now consider constitutions conducive to nonkilling societies. If Machiavelli can prescribe skills for violence-accepting dominance, it is now possible to work out the strategy and tactics of nonviolent political power. If Hobbes can propose a monster state coercing social peace by a monopoly of violence, new modes of governance responsive to human needs can be explored where no lethality is needed. If Locke can envision violent revolution to displace despotic rule, we can now perceive the strategy and tactics of nonviolent democratic liberation. If Marx and Engels can envision class struggle with violence as the ultimate arbiter, we can now envision processes of nonviolent struggle to realize age-old aspirations for economic justice. If Rousseau can prescribe a social contract based upon lethality against violators, and if present leaders continue to speak of violence-based "contracts" and "covenants," we can now begin to explore mutual commitments to well-being in nonkilling communities. If Kant (1795/1959) can envision "perpetual peace" deriving from steadfast adherence to a no-war categorical imperative, we can now perceive elements needed to transform a nonkilling imperative into global reality. If the American political tradition bequeaths a classic declaration of violent independence and a violence-affirming constitution, it is now possible to envision a nonviolent declaration of independence from American societal violence and a new nonkilling constitution. And if Weber can prescribe politics as a vocation that must accept the inevitability of violence, we can now envisage politics and political science as vocations that assume the possibility of liberation from violence (Arendt 1970; Muller and Semelin, 1995; Steger and Lind, 1999).

A nonkilling shift implies serious critical introduction of Gandhian political thought into the field of philosophy and theory. Its absence is akin to past failure to recognize Gandhi for the Nobel peace prize in a violence-affirming world. Resources abound for taking up the task, mainly by Indian interpreters from varied ideological and disciplinary perspectives together with pioneering non-Indian contributors (Dhawan 1957; Dange et al. 1977; Iyer 1973; Parekh 1989a, 1989b; Bondurant 1969; Dalton 1993; Galtung 1992; Sharp 1979; Steger 2000).

Opportunities for creative advancement of nonkilling theory are presented by the thought of proponents of nonviolent alternatives, past and present, in all world cultures. A survey from 550 B.C.E. is provided by Arthur and Lila Weinberg (1963). Multi-religious roots are set forth in T.K.N. Unnithan and Yogendra Singh (1973). In the Graeco-Roman, Euro-American tradition, Will Morrisey (1996) presents a massively erudite critique of pacifism since antiquity.

As global inquiries into nonviolent political thought are undertaken, some surprising discoveries can be expected. Such is the nonviolent definition of "politics" offered by the Korean political philosopher Hwang, Jang Yop during a December 3, 1987 interview in Pyongyang: "Politics means the harmonization of the interests of all members of society on the basis of love and equality." Both he and the interviewer were then unaware of the extraordinary studies by the sociologist Sorokin (1948; 1954) on "love" and "creative altruism" that can be combined with Arendt's (1970) emphasis upon conversing, deciding, and acting together and Burton's (1979) emphasis upon processes of responsiveness to human needs.

All can be seeds of new nonkilling political theory.

Polity Studies

In holistic studies of politically organized societies and their components, from villages to nation states and transnational entities—such as the field of American government and politics—the logic of nonkilling analysis raises questions that courageously need to be asked to overcome what futurist Harold Linstone has called the "assumption drag" of convention. Political lethality prefers to remain unquestioned within the citadel of patriotism. Where questions cannot be raised inside a polity, outside political scientists must take them up.

A nonkilling approach implies need to answer several questions. First, what has killing contributed to the formation and maintenance of each political society? To what extent does the polity's self-image rest upon a history of laudable lethality? What kinds of killing, governmental and nongovernmental, persist and what are their future prospects? How are citizens socialized to participate in and support killing, legal or extralegal, pro- or contra-governments, at home or abroad? How do political, economic, social, and cultural ideas, practices, and structures contribute to lethality? What influences does killing have upon the polity's ability to pursue other values, whether material or of the spirit such as freedom and equality?

Second, what are the historical roots of nonkilling ideas, practices, policies, and institutions in the society? What are their present manifestations and future prospects? What is the record of nonviolent resistance to violent political power? What is the record of creativity and constructive action toward realization of a nonkilling society?

A third requirement in polity studies is to question the record of transitions and reversals between killing and nonkilling. What significant figures, groups, and organizations have engaged in such transitions? Have soldiers become pacifists? Have killers converted to reverence for life? Have violent revolutionaries committed themselves to nonviolent social change? Have religious figures renounced the blessing of lethality? Have cultural figures shifted between acceptance and rejection of violence?

What changes have taken place in the range of offenses for which the death penalty has been imposed, abolished, or reinstated? Have military forces been demobilized and then revived? Have armies been abolished? Have police and citizens undergone disarmament and rearmament? Have there been instances of genuinely peaceful reconciliation between formerly deadly antagonists perhaps followed by re-eruptions of lethality? Have violence-supporting economies been shifted in whole or in part to respond to nonviolent individual and social needs?

Fourth, what are the historical and contemporary intra-polity elements—political, social, economic, and cultural—which if combined and expressed in nonviolent transitional processes show promise of realization *for that society* of desirable nonkilling conditions of life? What kinds of changes in religions, ideologies, laws, institutions, policies, socio-economic structures, education, communication, arts, and inter-polity relations would contribute to realization of a nonkilling society *in that context*? What conditions would best facilitate advancement of such values as freedom, equality, material well-being, and security without reversion to killing or threats to kill?

Comparative Politics

A nonkilling shift implies placing the question of nonviolent human capabilities at the center of comparative political inquiry. What insights can be gained by global comparison of the ideas, institutions, structures, processes, and policies that relate to removal of threat or use of lethal force by governments and citizens within and across societies? Guided by the logic of nonkilling analysis and the search for effective transformational practices, comparative inquiry seeks knowledge of alternatives beyond the bounds of the single polity.

Societies can be compared and ranked on propensities to kill or not to kill just as this has been done for democratic institutions, human rights, status of women, children's welfare, and levels of economic development. Among measures of lethality are killings by agents and antagonists of the state, criminal predation, citizen homicide and suicide, cross-state killing of members of other societies, professional training for killing, technological capabilities, and material indicators of the political economy of lethality. Parallel ranking can be made of nonkilling characteristics as derived from single polity analysis. Periodic comparative rankings of killer nations and nonkilling nations, should be a public service contribution of global political science. No less important than daily monitoring of global stock markets or sports scores, should be reports of rising and falling levels of lethality and of growth or repression of nonviolent transformational capabilities.

Cross-polity as well as intra-polity comparisons of societal components under most-similar or least similar conditions are needed to assist causal and transformational understanding. These include lethal and nonviolent propensities of religions, ideologies, arts, parties, genders, age cohorts, education levels, classes, ethnic groups, economic enterprises, universities, and professions.

Nonkilling comparative studies are needed to advance the contemporary political science thesis that democratic states as compared with authoritarian regimes do not go to war against each other and kill fewer of their own citizens. The persistence of killing within and by liberal democracies, whether presidential or parliamentary in structure, accompanied by manifest cultures of violence highlights the importance of comparative studies for insights into nonkilling structural and cultural alternatives. For example, as observed in Chaper 2, a comparative study of two proximate Mexican villages, ranking high and low in violence but otherwise similar in socioeconomic conditions, found cultural self-image to be a differentiating characteristic. The violent villagers saw themselves as violent and accepted it. The nonviolent villagers perceived themselves as peaceful and took pride in it (Fry 1994). A comparative study of children's play in two Indonesian villages, one high and one low in violence, found that the more violent culture favored games of human and animal combat. The less violent culture engaged in games of euphoria, such as swinging on vines, and in peaceful emulation of adult and animal behavior (Royce 1980). Such findings assist insight into the violent cultural correlates of competitive contact sports like boxing, hockey, wrestling, and American football.

International Politics

A nonkilling shift simultaneously introduces concern for the whole and for the individual in the field variously termed international politics, international relations, or world politics. It combines macroscopic and microscopic inquiry with customary concern for intermediate institutions. On the one hand, components of the global polity (state and non-state), structures of relationships among them, and processes of problem-solving are viewed as a whole. This does not mean to be ahistorical or non-contextual. The history is of humankind. The context is the pattern of interdependent interactions among global and local conditions.

On the other hand, the assumed realizability of a nonkilling global society requires attention to the well-being of each individual who shares life on earth from birth to death as generations come, intermingle, and pass on. The basic unit of nonkilling political analysis is the individual human being. Organizations, structures, and processes are the product of aggregated individual behavior. World politics is the politics of world individuals. A nonkilling global society depends upon individuals who do not kill. If no one is to kill or be killed, the interests of all human beings must be taken into account.

This implies the need to apply the logic of nonkilling analysis and action to global humanity as a whole. For violence, it means to extend the political science tradition of research on state violence, anti-state violence, and war to include all forms of lethality within and between societies—and to aggregate them in global patterns of causal explanation. For nonviolence, it means to identify nonkilling forces within and across political entities on a global scale. For nonviolent transformation it means to understand processes of interaction between killing and nonkilling forces within and across societies in a global general systems context.

For comprehensive understanding of practical, possible, and desirable features of a nonkilling global society, inquiry is needed into past and present social manifestations and aspirations, assuming theoretically infinite variations within a nonkilling whole. At the individual level it means to understand violent and nonviolent propensities of individuals, the dynamics of their nonviolent transformations, and the characteristics of social contexts supportive of lifelong expressions of creative individual nonviolent potential.

In applied orientations to change the funnel of lethality into a fan of nonlethal alternatives, a global perspective means to seek holistic killing zone interventions that supersede suppressive lethal practices. It means to contribute to global socialization and training of leadership and citizenship for nonkilling problem-solving. It means to identify and encourage global cultural contributions to nonkilling change. And it means to understand and assist nonviolent global changes in political, military, economic, social, and cultural structures that support lethality.

Nonkilling Political Science

Proceeding from the assumption that humans are capable of creating killing-free societies raises questions for every field, subfield, and aspect of contemporary political science. Assuming that political science cannot be value-free, is nonkilling an acceptable disciplinary value? Can the theory and practice of nonkilling political power successfully contend with and transform violent conceptions and manifestations? Are nonkilling democratic institutions from local to global possible? Can transitions from violent national security to nonviolent national and global security be made? From violent political economies to nonviolent global political economy? Can contributions to nonkilling theory and practice be made from perspectives such as feminism, race, class, ethnicity, language, and religion? And what methodologies are best suited for comprehensive understanding of societal violence, nonviolent potentials, transformative processes, and of ways to project and monitor stable yet creatively diverse nonkilling outcomes?

This is not to imply absence of political science contributions in every field that bear upon these questions. But it is to invite thought about what political science would be like if it took seriously the possibility of realizing nonkilling societies in a nonkilling world. Acceptance of such a possibility implies active political science engagement in nonviolent global problem-solving.

Chapter 4

PROBLEM-SOLVING IMPLICATIONS

> All of those who denounce and combat this holocaust [of tens of millions of deaths from malnutrition and economic deprivation] are unanimous in maintaining that the causes of this tragedy are political.
>
> Manifesto of Fifty-three Nobel Laureates 1981

What are the problem-solving implications of nonkilling political science?

The overall goal is to end lethality in global life. This implies special concern for the lifelong well-being of every human being as potential victim or killer. It makes interest in individuals and creative purposiveness central to political science. On the other hand, it implies problem-solving engagement that recognizes yet transcends each spiritual, gender, age, ethnic, class, professional, national, or political identity. It implies nonviolent "multiple loyalties" (Guetzkow 1955) combined with transcendent commitment to facilitate processes of problem-solving that respond to the needs of all without threat or use of lethal force.

Nonkilling political science implies simultaneous commitment to decrease factors conducive to lethality and to strengthen those that favor nonviolence. It seeks to solve problems within and across all five zones of the convergent funnel of lethality (Figure 1) and fan of nonkilling alternatives

(Figure 2). It means direct engagement by the profession of political science as a whole in acceptance of problem-solving responsibilities and indirect support of the efforts of others. It includes facilitation of research and training to assist public and private problem-solving action. It means to facilitate participation by all in need-satisfying processes of individual and social decision-making.

To accept a problem-solving role for nonkilling political science does not imply omniscience, omnicompetence, or omnipotence. But it does imply potential relevance for well-being in all areas of social life—spiritual, physical, material, and cultural. This does not mean totalitarian intervention, but rather recognition that what political figures, institutions, governments, and people who support them do or fail to do have far-reaching social consequences from physical survival through economic well-being to the highest reaches of human aspiration. In seeking to be of service to nonkilling societies, political science need not be more restrictive in the potential breadth of its concerns and contributions than the professions of medicine and public health.

Problems may be defined as dissonance between the desirable and the actual. Every problem presents complex sub-problems of indeterminacy: *normative* (what should be), *empirical* (what is), and *potential* (what can be). Each problem further embodies systemic complexities, mutually dependent feedback processes, and past-present-future time components. But however difficult and complex problems may be—ethically, philosophically, or empirically—nonkilling political science does not disavow explicit engagement in efforts to solve those that threaten the survival and well-being of humankind. Nonkilling political science engages in efforts to end behavioral violence, to change conditions of structural violence, and to solve problems of both in interaction. It seeks to remove support for lethality, to assist existing institutions for nonkilling service, and to create new nonkilling policies and institutions.

In accepting an applied science and applied humanities problem-solving role for political science, it is unscientific to require that solutions must be known in advance. Neither the assumption that diseases are incurable nor that cures must be known in advance of diagnosis, prescription, and treatment prevents progress in basic and applied medical science. Political science, at base also a matter of life and death, need not be different.

It is not reasonable to expect nonkilling political science to demonstrate instant solutions to problems that violence-accepting politics and political science have not been able to solve. Vast commitments of scientific, human, and material resources to suppress violence by violent means accompanied by incredible bloodshed have not succeeded in putting an end to global lethality, from war and genocide to homicide in capitals of nuclear weapon states. Enormous creativity has been devoted to killing. No less inventiveness will be needed to demonstrate nonkilling alternatives that work.

To end the era of human lethality, of course, is not a task for political science alone. It is shared by all sciences, humanities, professions, and by everyone. But it is a task in which political science can take initiatives as well as support the initiatives of others. Priority tasks are to solve problems customarily taken to be so formidable as to negate any possibility of creating a nonkilling political science in service to a nonkilling world. Three are generic: the problems of "hitler and the holocaust," revolutionary structural change, and security from the individual to the nation-state.

Nonkilling, Hitler and the Holocaust

The problem of political leadership and lethality—exemplified but not limited to the generic example of hitler and the holocaust—must be confronted directly and subjected to sustained basic and applied science problem-solving efforts. The horrendous examples of genocidal aggression, mass class exterminations, and civic annihilations must not be allowed to paralyze nonkilling scientific creativity. Otherwise political science is forever fated, explicitly or implicitly, to prepare for countervailing murderousness, violence greater than that of which any genocidal dictator, revolutionary class exterminator, or righteous annihilator of cities and villages is capable.

A practical way to begin is to intensify interdisciplinary work in the still underdeveloped field of political leadership studies. This means to identify lethality-prone behavioral and systemic variables and to seek changes conducive to realization of nonkilling leadership and followership. Some variables already identified as capable of purposive, nonkilling transformative interventions are violence-prone concepts of leadership; personality prerequisites; role powers; organizational supports; task expectations; value saliencies; technological capabilities; and economic, social, and cultural reinforcements for killing (Paige 1977).

Twentieth century experience suggests some points of departure. To stop the respective emergence of killing-prone leaders supported by killing-prone followers, at some point in history humans must simply refuse to kill and refuse to cooperate with systems that kill. Otherwise cycles of lethality between vengeful vanquished and traumatized victors will continue. This seems simplistic. But in retrospect twentieth century atrocities show that late nineteenth century peace advocates who sought to abolish war were completely correct. There is a clear connection among atrocities from World War I to World War II to the Cold War and beyond. A preventive political science contribution is to identify and help to reconcile vengeful animosities, however recent or ancient, before they erupt in atrocities. To stop the rise of leaders and followers who celebrate vengeful extermination of enemies, political science must clearly commit itself to prevent killing, to reconcile the vengeful, and to create conditions of nonkilling life.

To stop the rise of potential hitlers, stalins, maos, amins, pol pots, or even atomic-bombing trumans: redefine the concept of political leadership from that of lethal commander to facilitator of nonkilling societal problem-solving; seek early identification of and withdraw support from leader aspirants with aggressive, violence-prone personalities; remove expectations of willingness to kill and power to order others to kill from leadership role responsibilities; do not provide leaders with professional killer organizations pledged to obedience and armed with increasingly lethal weapons; withdraw religious, business, labor, scientific, and artistic support for killing-prone organizations and commit to nonkilling alternatives; elevate need-responsive conflict resolution to be a primary task expectation of political leaders and citizens; affirm commitment to the value of nonkilling as a core component of national pride and identity; refuse definition of any group as subhuman or otherwise so evil as to justify extermination; seek common dialogue among groups for mutual well-being; change socioeconomic and other structural conditions that predispose individuals and groups directly or vicariously to seek satisfaction by violence; shift the economy of killing to serve life-affirming human needs; and support creation of nonkilling cultures through arts and sciences.

Killing-zone interventions against hitler-type atrocities, of course, pose an even greater challenge to applied nonkilling scientific creativity. But they are not unthinkable, especially in an age of unprecedented capacity for technological innovation. Measures to be considered and tested in problem-solving simulations include microscopic and mass evocation of leader-follower, spiritual-psychological, nonkilling capabilities-inhibitions; global condemnation of, withdrawal of support from, and resistance to killing (not burden of victims alone); provisions for rapid exodus; and space-air-sea-ground interventions by forces equipped with sophisticated techniques for incapacitating individuals, groups, and technologies that kill. Focus comprehensively emergency interventionary pressures, direct and multi-channeled, negative and positive, upon sources of lethality as identified for prevention.

In the aftermath of hitler-type traumatizations, transformative affirmation of nonkilling human capabilities among survivors—killers, victims, and relatives—must be sought. Political science must be engaged in creating processes for recognition of responsibility for atrocity, restitution, reconciliation, and most importantly facilitating preventive and structural changes that favor realization of nonkilling societies in a nonkilling world. Drawing upon every source of spirit, science, and tradition—nonkilling must be celebrated as the heart of future cultural identity and pride among peoples. Practical commitments must be made to ensure that such atrocities will never happen again.

To end the era of mass atrocities from genocide to war, nonkilling political science must engage in three applied science tasks: prevention, intervention, and post-traumatic nonkilling transformation. It must liberate itself from the barrier to creative service imposed by the conventional assumption that such atrocities cannot be eliminated on nonkilling principles.

Nonkilling and Violent Revolution

A second major problem to engage problem-solving efforts is that of violent revolution and counterrevolution. Related are military coups, countercoups, terrorism, counterterrorism, guerilla war, and large scale civil war. Conventional political science tends to regard such revolutions and their repression with violence-accepting ambiguity. Violence against bad regimes but not good regimes is laudable. Counterviolence against bad revolutionaries but not good revolutionaries is acceptable. In either case violence to achieve or resist political change is a seemingly intractable and often meritorious fact of political life. Familiar arguments among some American scholars, for example, have been that since economic elites will not relinquish property and power peacefully, revolutionary violence is justified. Others, however, support counterviolence against rebels who seek to change systems of private property exploitation. The idea that one must always be prepared for revolutionary lethality persists even under conditions of American electoral democracy in insistence by some upon citizen gun possession for defense of liberty against the state.

But assuming needs for removing repressive political regimes and for changing intolerable conditions of socioeconomic structural violence, nonkilling political science can assist in identifying and assisting nonviolent revolutionary alternatives. This requires challenging the assumption that revolutions must necessarily be violent and providing knowledge of effective nonviolent alternatives: principles, strategies, tactics, organizational methods, and implementing skills.

During the last half of the Cold War, three remarkable affirmations of the possibility of nonviolent revolution by political theorists arose from three of the world's most influential violent revolutionary traditions: the United States, the Soviet Union, and China. In the United States, Gene Sharp (1973) presented a classic statement of theory and practice for nonviolent political revolutions rooted in penetrating analysis of the acquiescent bases of political power and wide-ranging historical inquiry into examples of effective nonviolent struggle. Sharp identified at least 198 methods of nonviolent action: from protest and persuasion; through social, economic, and political noncooperation; to direct nonviolent intervention. He then proceeded to combine all in a dynamic theory of nonviolent transformation involving processes of "conversion, accommodation, and coercion" to which he later added "disintegration." In the Soviet Union, E. G. Plimak and Y. F. Karyakin (1979) defined revolution as a shift in state power from one class to another that produces a "sharp change in the life of the vast mass of the people." Then they argued on the basis of Marxist-Leninist theory and post-WWII decolonizing and democratic experience that peaceful socialist revolutions were possible. They defined a peaceful socialist revolution as one "without armed struggle, without civil war, and without armed counterrevolutionary intervention." Arguing that past failures should not deter pursuit of peaceful revolutions in new historical circumstances, they urged that possibilities for "peaceful revolutionary development . . . must be scrupulously and objectively studied in every aspect" (my translation). In China, Zhang Yi-Ping (1981: 79), basing his argument on Marxist theory and successful nonviolent struggles for national independence in Asia, Africa, and Latin America—especially upon mass mobilization capabilities demonstrated by the Gandhian movement in India—argued: "The view that one-sidedly advocates violent revolution without regard for time, place, and situation, and deprecates nonviolent revolution is *wrong in theory and harmful in practice*" (emphasis added, my translation).

Thus in a period of complex global revolutionary and counterrevolutionary bloodshed, political analysts emerging out of three violent traditions—independently and seemingly unknown to each other—set forth the scientific task of developing nonviolent revolutionary theory and practice. A noteworthy common element among them was reference to the nonviolent Gandhian movement in India that sought not only political independence but socioeconomic and cultural change.

Hitherto nonviolent revolutionary theory whether from "capitalist" or "socialist" standpoints has been conceived largely from the perspective of the oppressed. Comparable theories of nonviolent elite counteraction have not been developed to provide alternatives to violent repression of nonviolent revolutionary action. A reversal of Sharpian analysis is implied. Do the wealthy property owners, the ethnic dominants, the political leaders, the police, and the military have the theory and courage to face nonviolently and unarmed—the poor, the landless, the suppressed, the minorities or majorities—who are nonviolently asserting their claims to human rights and economic justice? Can the advantaged advance their counterclaims for dignity and recognition in actions seeking conversion, accommodation, and coercion without bloodshed?

Moreover an applied theory of "nonviolent struggle" or even "nonviolent class struggle" to bring about social transformations marked by mutually satisfactory relationships among former oppressors/advantaged and oppressed/disadvantaged is plausible. This can be inferred from nonkilling elements evokable in human nature and from repressive hostility expressed toward proponents of peaceful change by proviolent elites and their proviolent antagonists. Each combatant tends to repress proponents of nonviolent action on grounds that such ideas weaken the militant readiness to kill of their own support base/class. For example, during Cold War confrontation both American and Soviet elites and media were quick to discredit or stifle pacifist voices, implying that nonkilling ideas would evoke receptive responses and undermine support for their own militarism—not that they would weaken their opponents. Similarly academic and activist proponents of armed resistance movements are quick to denounce exploration of nonviolent revolutionary alternatives—implying fear of receptivity to nonkilling alternatives among the oppressed. Thus if there is receptivity to nonkilling principles and practices among both oppressors and oppressed, a nonkilling class struggle is contemplable. This implies an applied role for political science to facilitate nonkilling revolutionary problem-solving processes. Demonstrated effectiveness of emphasis upon the ultimate goal of "reconciliation" with adversaries at every stage of nonviolent struggle for social change that is characteristic of both Gandhian and Kingian methods provides a practical point of departure. Even Machiavelli has argued that profound changes in political regime from "tyranny to freedom" and vice versa can be achieved "without bloodshed" when realized by "general consent of the citizens who have made the state great" (*The Discourses,* Book 3, Chapter 7).

Nonkilling and Security

Nonkilling political science must solve the problem of providing credible security alternatives against lethal aggression at the individual, local, national and international levels. Conventional security theory and practice ultimately derive from the threat of lethality: "I/we want to make it absolutely credible to you that I/we will kill you." Nonkilling security, however, departs from the contrary principle; "I/we want to make it absolutely credible to you that I/we will not kill you. And you must make it absolutely credible that you will not kill me/us." In short, "We must make it absolutely credible to each other that we will not kill." No one is safe as long as someone is determined to kill them. Lethal ingenuity overcomes every defense from shields, armor, moats, walls, and castles to atomic bomb shelters. Offensive lethality overcomes every form of lethal defense: arrows over spears, machine guns over muskets, artillery over infantry, tanks over cavalry, rockets over tanks, submarines over battleships, air and missile forces over nearly everything, nuclear, biological, and chemical weapons over all. To live in an armored house filled with guns does not ensure security: the intruder may have armor-piercing missiles, heavier artillery, and greater combat skill—or simply ability to poison air, food, or the water supply. The only certain security is absence of the will to kill.

The role of political science in transition to nonlethal security is to help develop theory and practice to provide credible alternatives to threat or use of lethal force—including preventive nonlethal transformation of the will to kill among potential adversaries. Although hitherto not salient in conventional political science, a growing body of literature and experience provides a basis from which to advance. Explorations include inquiries into civilian resistance to Nazi genocide (Hallie 1979; Fogelman 1994; Semelin 1994); Danilo Dolci's nonviolent community resistance to mafia criminality (Amato 1979; Chaudhuri

1998); unarmed bodyguards for human rights workers (Mahony and Eguren 1997); nonviolent resistance to military coups (Roberts 1975; Sharp 1990; 1993); nonviolent national, civilian, social defense (Boserup and Mack 1974; Sharp 1990; Martin et al. 1991; Randle 1993; Burrowes 1996); nonlethal uses of conventional military forces (Keyes 1982); alternative nonviolent forces (Banerjee 2000; Weber 1996; Moser-Puangsuwan and Weber 2000); and the development of nonlethal weapons (Lewer and Schofield 1997).

Several governments have undertaken feasibility studies of nonviolent civilian defense, albeit as a complement to conventional military means. Among them are Sweden, Norway, Denmark, Netherlands, France, Latvia, Lithuania, Estonia, Austria, Switzerland, and Finland (Schmid 1985; Sharp, 1990; Randle 1994: 121–37). In Thailand a unique, preemptive provision to legitimate nonviolent resistance to future military coups has been included in Article 65 of the new Thai Constitution of 1997: "People have the right peacefully to oppose any attempt to seek administrative power by means which are not stipulated by the Constitution."

Research on nonlethal weapons for police and military use has been undertaken in the United States at least since 1965, and accelerated in the 1990s. A wide range of technologies have been explored—including laser, optical, acoustical, electromagnetic pulse, chemical, biological, and dozens of other weapons. Some have already been used in police and overseas military operations (Lewer and Schofield 1997). Like governmental interest in social defense, interest in nonlethal weapons is presently regarded as a complement to conventional lethal capabilities. But the fact that nonkilling alternatives are being taken seriously by traditional experts in violent security should encourage no less serious and even more advanced comprehensive efforts by political science. The challenge is to solve problems of transition to completely nonkilling security conditions. A further sign of movement toward nonlethal security is contained in the final report of the

Carnegie Commission on Preventing Deadly Conflict (1997) which calls for "structural prevention: strategies to address the root causes of deadly conflict," as well as creation of a "culture of prevention." The possibility of taking further steps toward nonkilling individual and global security is implied. The proposal to organize a Global Nonviolent Peace Force is an example (www.nonviolentpeaceforce.org).

Nonkilling political science must seek solutions to problems hitherto deemed insuperable obstacles to realization of nonviolent societies. Overcoming direct threats of extinction by aggressive physical violence must be of paramount concern. First, because without survival no other problem can be solved. Second, because continued commitment to killing contributes to conditions of structural and ecological violence that threaten individual, societal, and planetary well-being.

The emphasis upon nonkilling as an approach to societal problem-solving confronts questions such as the following: why concentrate attention on nonkilling when psychological abuse, torture, racism, sexism, economic exploitation, and dictatorships inflict more suffering and deaths than physical lethality? These questions imply that such problems can only be solved if we maintain the option to kill. One answer is that the will, capability, and culture of killing is a major underlying cause of socioeconomic structural inequities that kill and psychophysical abuses that temporarily stop short of killing. How can abuse, torture, racism, oppression of women, economic exploitation, and dictatorship endure if not based upon fear and threat of death? The removal of killing from homicide to war from human experience will contribute substantially—spiritually, psychologically, materially, democratically, and environmentally—to solving other problems that confront humankind.

Commitment to nonkilling implies political science engagement in helping to solve characteristic problems of each era that threaten human survival and well-being. Speaking to villages, Gandhi used to check off on the fingers of his left hand the principal problem-solving tasks: equality for untouchables; self-reliant spinning of cotton cloth for economic liberation; abstention from drugs and alcohol; Hindu-Muslim friendship; and equality for women. Then he would say, "And the wrist is non-violence" (Ashe 1969: 243). Analogously we can engage five problems that are now globally salient: continued killing and the need for disarmament; the holocaust of poverty and the need for economic equity; violations of human dignity and needs for mutual respect of human rights; destruction of the biosphere and the need for planetary life-support; and other-denying divisiveness that impedes problem-solving cooperation.

These five problems are common to the individual, family, community, nation, and to humankind as a whole. We all need freedom from being killed, from economic deprivation, from denial of dignity, from a poisoned environment, and from failures to cooperate in solving these and other problems. These problems are interrelated and are exacerbated by continued reliance upon lethality as the ultimate problem-solver. We seek security by killing and arming to kill, creating counter-killing threats; arming to kill contributes to economic deprivation and reinforces structural inequity; killing in assertion and denial of human rights contributes to long-festering retaliatory resentments; lethal combat and military industrialization ravage the environment; and fearful compartmentalization in antagonistic enclaves impedes the development of problem-solving cooperation to benefit all.

Nonkilling problem-solving implies not only negation of killing but constructive engagement in need-fulfilling change. This means unequivocal engagement in abolition of war and its weapons, abolition of poverty, nonviolent expression of human rights and responsibilities, proactive promotion of environmental sustainability, and contribution to problem-solving processes that respond to human needs and evoke infinite creative potential in individuals and in humankind as a whole.

Such an agenda may seem utopian. But it is bequeathed by some of the most practically experienced political, military, economic, scientific, cultural, and civil society leaders of this era (echoing ancient human concerns in a new global age). It is extremely important for political scientists to note that virtually every major problem-solving conference convened under the auspices of the United Nations or other bodies calls for the peoples of the world to help create the "political will" to bring about needed change. Calls go out not only to governments but to all sources of cooperative problem-solving action: parties, nongovernmental organizations, corporations, unions, universities, the media, religions, and the arts. There is a sense of increasing urgency as life-threatening global problems intensify and awareness grows of catastrophic future consequences of present failure to act. These include the proliferation of weapons; rapidly increasing populations combined with widening economic disparities within and between nations that threaten to burst material and psychological limits of tolerance; life-threatening effects of unrestrained industrial and agricultural exploitation of nature; and self-defeating failure to honor the claims to equal participation in realizing acceptable quality of life for all by women, indigenous peoples, suppressed minorities, and those of myriad cultural identities. For those most knowledgeable about the global condition—as opposed to a global view from the perspective of a single nation-state—such as Federico Mayor, Director General of UNESCO—it is an urgent era of "no business as usual" (Mayor 1995: 83–93). Should it be less urgent for political science?

Nonkilling and Disarmament

Neither the problems to be solved nor the nonviolent movements that have arisen to address them are academic political science inventions. They are presented by contemporary global political life. Political science should commit itself to solve them. A clear-cut challenge for problem-solving action is contained in the *Final Report* of the first U.N. General Assembly special session on disarmament (U.N. General Assembly 1978) that calls for "general and complete disarmament under effective international control." By consensus, 159 states with one abstention (Albania) declared the need for abolition of all nuclear weapons; abolition of all biochemical weapons and other weapons of mass destruction; withdrawal from all foreign military bases; reduction of armed forces to purposes of limited territorial defense; reduction of conventional weapons; and ending "colossal waste" in global military expenditures by shifting material and human resources to serve economic and social needs in more and less economically developed countries. Plus many related proposals. A classic call for nonviolent transformative action by predominantly violent states, unfortunately unknown to most students of political science.

Nonkilling political science cannot remain aloof from efforts to support governmental and civil society initiatives that promise evolution toward realization of weapon-free societies. Among them are campaigns to ban handguns, assault weapons, land mines, and the arms trade; to establish weapon-free zones of peace in villages and cities; and to create nuclear-weapon-free regions of the world.

Nonkilling and Economic Deprivation

Yet another classic appeal for problem-solving action is the "Manifesto" of fifty-three Nobel Prize laureates from chemistry to physics to stop what they call the global "holocaust" of deaths from preventable economic deprivation (Nobel Prize Winners 1981: 61–3).[10] They declare: "All who denounce and combat this holocaust are unanimous in maintaining that the causes of this tragedy are political."

> It is essential that citizens and politicians choose and vote at their respective levels, in elections, in parliament, in govern-

> ments or at the international level, new laws, new budgets, new projects and new measures designed to take immediate effect to save billions of people from malnutrition and underdevelopment and hundreds of millions in every generation from death by hunger (62).

Expressing "the need to save the living, not to kill and not to exterminate, not even by inertia, failure to act or indifference," they urge transformative nonviolent economic revolution:

> Although the powerful of this earth bear the greatest responsibility, they are not alone. If the helpless take their fate into their own hands, if increasing numbers refuse to obey any law other than fundamental human rights, the most basic of which is the right to life, if the weak organize themselves and use the few but powerful weapons available to them: *non-violent actions exemplified by Gandhi* (emphasis added), adopting and imposing objectives which are limited and suitable: if these things happen it is certain that an end could be put to this catastrophy in our time (63).

They conclude, "Now is the time to act, now is the time to create, now is the time for us to live in a way that will give life to others."

Inequality, population growth, and militarization interact to exacerbate economic lethality, violence, and environmental devastation. In 1999 the World Bank estimated that perhaps as many as 1.5 billion people are living in conditions of "absolute poverty," defined as having income of less than $1 per day, with 3 billion under $2 per day. In India alone it is estimated that the absolute poor have increased from 300 million persons to 340 million since the late 1980s (World Bank 1999). Simultaneously income inequality increases. As summarized by Tariq Husain of the World Bank in June 1997 for 160 young leaders in the first program of the United Nations University International Leadership Academy:

> The world in mid-1990s is . . . more polarized than in 1980 . . . . The poorest 20% of the world's people have seen their share of global income decline from 2.3% to 1.4% during the past 30 years. Meanwhile, for the richest, it rose from 70% to 85%. Thus the ratios of the shares of the richest and poorest doubled from 30:1 to 61:1 . . . . The combined assets of the world's 360 billionaires now exceeds the combined annual income of countries with 45% of the world's peoples (Husain 1997: 13).

The World Bank President James D. Wolfensohn and Mahatma Gandhi agree that inequality leads to violence. The President observes, "Inequality leads to instability. Poverty breeds war" (Husain 1997: 6). As the Mahatma warns, "A non-violent system of government is clearly an impossibility so long as a wide gulf between the rich and hungry millions persists . . . . A violent and bloody revolution is a certainty one day unless there is voluntary abdication of riches and power that riches give and sharing them for the common good" (*Collected Works* 75 (1941): 158). Combining insights of the President and the Mahatma, a young American peace worker, Betsy Duren, who has given away most of her inherited wealth, declares: "The only way we're going to have lasting peace is by redistributing wealth. Poverty, war and suffering are caused by people who have more than their share of the pie trying to hold on to it" (Mogil and Slepian 1992: 100). The views of the President, the Mahatma, and the young American echo the analysis of Aristotle over 2,300 years ago on the relation of inequality to lethality:

> The important thing to remember is that those who are responsible for the exercise of power, whether they be individuals or organs of government or tribes or what you will, great or small, it is they who cause the disturbance that leads to revolution.

> They may do so indirectly, as when the rest, jealous of their power, begin a revolution, but also directly when they themselves are so superior that they are no longer content to remain on terms of equality with the rest (Aristotle 1962: 199).

Rapid global population growth from 2.5 billion in 1950 to estimated 6.1 billion in 2000 and 8.9 billion in 2050 challenges nonviolent problem-solving engagement. The most populous countries in 2050 are predicted to be India (1,529,000,000), China (1,478,000,000), the United States (349,000,000), Pakistan (345,000,000), and Indonesia (321,000,000). As analyzed by Lester R. Brown and colleagues of the Worldwatch Institute, such unprecedented increase of at least 80 million people each year places potentially catastrophic demands upon the life-carrying capacity of the earth. Among nineteen areas of threatening concern are water supply, grain production, energy, cropland, forests, biodiversity, climate change, disease, urbanization, housing, education, jobs, and conflict within and among countries (Brown, Gardner, and Halweil 1999).

Since traditional lethal methods of population reduction such as war, genocide, infanticide, and abortion as well as famine and pestilence are undesirable, the challenge to nonkilling political science is to support discovery and implementation of nonviolent alternatives. This means placing respect for the quality of human life and its life-supporting environment at the center of political theory and practice in economic problem-solving.

Some of the world's most celebrated military leaders, professionals in killing, have demonstrated acute insight into the need for economic demilitarization. One of them is the WWII general who became president of the United States, Dwight D. Eisenhower (1953–1961). No pacifist has surpassed his succinct and powerful analysis of the nexus between commitment to killing and economic structural violence:

> Every gun that is made, every warship launched, every rocket fired signifies, in the final sense, a theft from those who hunger and are not fed, those who are cold and not clothed. This world in arms is not spending money alone. It is spending the sweat of its laborers, the genius of its scientists, the hopes of its children . . . . This is not a way of life at all, in any true sense. Under the cloud of threatening war, it is humanity hanging from a cross of iron. (Address to the American Society of Newspaper Editors, April 16, 1953).

One reason for humanity's "hanging from a cross of iron," is the "theft" by cost of the United States nuclear weapons program from 1940 to 1996 calculated to be 5.821 trillion dollars (Schwartz 1998). This exemplifies the "colossal waste" of global military expenditures that in the 1990s averaged "well over $500 billion a year" (Sivard 1996: 7). Nonkilling political science implies refusal to accept continuation of economic deprivation caused by global militarization. It accepts constructive engagement in efforts to free humanity from the "cross of iron" to end the "holocaust" of poverty.

Nonkilling Human Rights and Responsibilities

An imperative challenge to problem-solving engagement is posed by the Universal Declaration of Human Rights (1948) and its subsequent implementing covenants, civil and political, social and economic. The basic text should be known to every political scientist and global citizen.

However human rights are defined, amidst controversies over universality versus cultural specificity, nonkilling political science is committed to their assertion and defense by nonviolent means. Moreover, it asserts the goal of obtaining and implementing universal recognition of the right not to be killed and the responsibility not to kill others. One way is to seek inclusion in the Universal Declaration and in global practice of the following provision:

> Article 3(2). Everyone has the right not to be killed and the responsibility not to kill others.

Nonkilling political science is challenged to engage its resources in research, training, consultation and action to support individuals and organizations that seek the protection and advancement of human rights at every level. For example, the program of action to end all forms of violence against women and girls set forth by the 1995 Beijing women's conference presents a compelling agenda for implementational commitment (United Nations 1996).

Another challenge to full-scale political science engagement is nonviolent defense of human rights by Amnesty International founded in 1961. Its work is based on Universal Declaration principles such as "No one shall be subjected to torture or to cruel, inhuman or degrading treatment or punishment" (Art. 5); "No one shall be subjected to arbitrary arrest, detention or exile" (Art. 9); and "Everyone has the right to freedom of opinion and expression; this right includes freedom to hold opinions without interference and to seek receive and impart information and ideas through any media and regardless of frontiers" (Art. 18). Amnesty International seeks global abolition of the death penalty, abolition of torture, fair trials for all, and immediate release of all prisoners of conscience who have neither advocated nor engaged in violence. Methods encompass all forms of nonviolent political action.

Among other human rights work that should engage nonkilling political science assistance is that of the Unrepresented Nations and Peoples Organization (UNPO), founded in 1991. UNPO seeks recognition of the collective human rights of more than fifty indigenous peoples on five continents. Members commit themselves in writing to the UNPO Covenant that provides for "promotion of non-violence and the rejection of terrorism as an instrument of policy." UNPO calls upon "governments, international organizations, NGOs and on their leaders to adopt clear and principled policies to reduce the use of violence." These must include:

> recognition of and respect for the equal rights of all peoples and those of minorities, regardless of their size, their culture or religion; taking the needs and views of unrepresented peoples and minorities seriously; speaking out and condemning all unprovoked acts of violence and gross violations of human rights against unrepresented peoples and minorities; recognition of the legitimacy of movements or governments which use peaceful and democratic means to achieve their objectives; engagement in open and sincere dialogue with all such movements and governments and rewarding their adherence to non-violence; (and) encouragement and active assistance in the peaceful resolution of conflicts between the State governments and nations, peoples and minorities over whom they claim authority (UNPO 1998: 8).

Furthermore, UNPO calls upon "corporations and financial institutions to end the violent exploitation of those resources upon which peoples' survival depends; and cease from promoting violence through irresponsible arms trade and commercialization of violence in the media and in their products" (9). Such commitment to nonviolent politics by peoples who have suffered genocide, ethnocide, and ecocide presents a clear challenge to supportive nonkilling political science. Given the large number and identity needs of the world's indigenous and minority peoples, the membership of UNPO eventually may exceed that of state members of the United Nations.

Nonkilling and Ecological Viability

Nonkilling political science implies assistance to liberation of humankind from ecological lethality. We kill the environment and the environment kills us. A nonkilling society requires a nonkilling ecology.

The end of the twentieth century has been marked by increasing alarm over human destruction of the life-carrying capacity of the biosphere. Military industrialization and assaults upon the planet in warfare contribute to its devastation. The World Charter for Nature adopted by 111 members of the U.N. General Assembly on October 28, 1982 declared that "nature shall be secured against degradation caused by warfare and other hostile activities" (Art. 1, Sect. 5). Among tragic violations: chemical defoliation of forests by the United States in the Vietnam War; Gulf War oil field arson by Iraq. Nonkilling political science confronts the challenge posed by Barry Commoner: "To make peace with the planet, we must make peace among the people who live in it" (Commoner 1990: 243).

Another challenge is posed by Maurice F. Strong, Secretary-General of the major United Nations Conference on Environment and Development held in Rio de Janeiro in 1992 who calls for an "eco-revolution that is essential in order to shift the world onto a new pathway to a more secure, sustainable and equitable future" (United Nations 1993: 1). *Agenda 21*, the call to action of the conference, observes that "warfare is especially destructive of sustainable development" (Principle 24) and that "peace, development and environmental protection are interdependent and indivisible" (Principle 25). Appeals for problem-solving action are addressed to states, governments, citizens, women, youth, and indigenous peoples. To which can be added armies, military industries, corporations, labor unions, and political scientists.

Like other threats to survival and well-being, ecological problems are complex, interdisciplinary, and global. Political science resources to assist public policy formulation and implementation need to be applied from a nonkilling perspective. The scientific task is to identify which environmental threats are well understood and require urgent action, which problems require urgent research, priorities among them, and how best to introduce scientific knowledge into need-responsive processes of societal decision-making. A model approach has been presented by the Royal Swedish Academy of Sciences (1983; Sebek 1983).

Nonkilling political science implies being especially attentive to and supportive of individuals, organizations, and social movements that engage in nonviolent environmental problem-solving action. Salient contemporary nonviolent ecological movements range from the village women's save-the-trees Chipko movement in India (Weber 1989; Nautiyal 1996), through direct action efforts to change public and private policies by Greenpeace (Stephenson 1997), to the emergence in Germany of an environmental movement and electoral political party, Die Grünen (The Greens).

The legacy of Petra Karin Kelly (1947–1992), a founder of the electoral Die Grünen, presents nonkilling political science with a problem-solving agenda for the twenty-first century. Her call to action encompasses every critical issue from disarmament through economy and human rights to worldwide cooperation to save the planet. She calls for a "global culture of ecological responsibility" and urges establishment of "binding principles governing ecological relations among all countries" (Kelly, 1992: 76). Along with Tolstoy, Gandhi, Abdul Ghaffar Khan, and Martin Luther King, Jr., Petra Kelly deserves to be seen now and will be recognized in the future as a major contributor to nonviolent global change in the twentieth century and beyond (Kelly 1989; 1992; 1994; Parkin 1994).

Nonkilling and Problem-Solving Cooperation

A generic task is to assist processes of peaceful problem-solving from individuals to the global community. Neither security, nor economic well-being, nor respect for human rights, nor ecological viability, nor other valued conditions of life can be achieved without life-respecting cooperation among all whose help is needed. This is not to imply that political science solves every problem but rather that it accepts responsibility to assist processes of problem-solving cooperation. It does not imply totalitarianism; even anarchists require cooperative respect for their freedoms by other anarchists. A nonkilling approach implies a shift from politics based upon conflict and competition for dominance with manifest or latent violence as the ultimate arbiter. Nonkilling politics implies ever-widening circles of cooperative problem-solving marked by life-celebrating mutual respect. Whereas violence dominates and divides, nonviolence cooperates and unites. Therefore nonkilling political science seeks coaction among men and women, religions, civilizations, races, ethnicities, classes, communities, states, national and transnational organizations, and global movements. The goal is to solve problems without killing or threat to kill for the well-being of all. The upsurge of interdisciplinary and professional interest in the theory and practice of conflict resolution, seeking win-win resolutions of conflicts through dialogue, provides major facilitating resources (Fisher and Ury 1981; Burton 1996).

Based upon advancing research, nonkilling political science engages in assisting transition toward nonkilling societies in states and civil societies characterized by violence. It recognizes historic advances of democratic development expressed in some modern political systems, but also seeks solutions to problems of behavioral and structural violence that free politics and free markets alone do not solve. Nonkilling political science recognizes the value of citizen-validated constitutions to limit arbitrary power; provision of bills of rights to secure citizen freedoms; the usefulness of institutional checks and balances of separated executive, legislative, and judicial authority; the substitution of electoral party competition for civil war; the services of a professional bureaucracy; religious freedom; freedom of press and expression; and expansion of rights of voting participation toward universal participation (Finer 1997; Goldman 1990). It further recognizes and seeks alternatives to the presence of violent military and police power that undergirds such systems, and that customarily has contributed to their establishment.

A nonkilling approach notes signs of systemic dysfunction in failures to respond to human needs that result in physical and structural violence in even the most "advanced" democracies. To recall just a few of current concern, taking the United States as an example: violence and homicide in family and school; youthful despair reflected in violent gangs, drugs, and suicide; pervasive political alienation, distrust of politics and government, expressed partly in low voting participation; immense waste of resources in unproductive military expenditure; a chronically deprived underclass of at least twenty percent of the population characterized by poor nutrition, health, housing (including homelessness), education, and family disintegration; armed robbery; hate crimes; gender and ethnic discrimination; a super affluent upper class of perhaps another twenty percent increasing in wealth and allied with proximate intermediate classes in seeking security through more police, prisons, severe punishments, and military force—all accompanied by violent cultural imagery.

Countries less characterized by attributes of the modern democratic state and civil society suffer even greater intensities and forms of violence associated with unrestrained lethal autocratic rule and economic deprivation resulting in unspeakable physical and structural atrocities. Among indicators are summary executions, torture, electoral assassinations, genocide, ethnocide, armed extortion, terrorism, armed revolutions, and mass deaths from state-backed economic deprivations.

Liberating itself from violence-accepting assumptions as to means and ends, the problem-solving task of nonkilling political science is to contribute to improved processes of responsiveness to human needs within and among societies that are more and less democratic. The challenge to scientific and humanist creativity is immense. Yet even now it is clear that contributions to constructive processual change can be made by explicit introduction of nonkilling values, provision of new information about nonkilling human capabilities, nurturance of new nonkilling skills of democratic leadership and citizenship, facilitation of participation in policy formation, and development of new nonlethal problem-solving institutions. To assist these changes, political science itself must clarify its commitment to nonkilling as a point of departure for service to society. It must become institutionally responsive to unmet human needs from the individual and family to the world polity.

Chapter 5

INSTITUTIONAL IMPLICATIONS

> That which we call necessary institutions are often no more than institutions to which we have grown accustomed, and . . . in matters of social constitution the field of possibilities is much more extensive than men living in their various societies are ready to imagine.
>
> Alexis de Tocqueville

> The problems that threaten life on Earth were produced collectively, they affect us collectively, and we must act collectively to change them.
>
> Petra K. Kelly

What are the institutional implications of a nonkilling ethical-empirical shift in political science? What does it imply for those who practice it, for the organization of the discipline, for its relation to other fields of knowledge, and for the varied institutions needed to bring about nonkilling societies from the local community to humankind as a whole? Institutions are taken to be configurations of purposive social relationships that arise in response to human needs and aspirations.

The history of civilization is in large part the history of institutional innovation. From faiths come communities associated in temples, synagogues, churches, and mosques. From needs for political participation come parties, elections, and parliaments. From needs for social control come police, courts, and prisons. From war-fighting objectives arise technological forces for combat on land, sea, and air. From needs for tax extraction to support armies and purposes of the state come bureaucracies (Finer 1997: 16-17, 20–21). To create an atomic bomb, national resources are mobilized in a Manhattan Project. To explore into realms unknown come the mobilizations of spirit, science, technology, skills, and resources to produce the fifteenth century voyages of Prince Henry the Navigator and the twentieth century Apollo Project to place a man on the moon.

For political science to contribute to transition to a nonkilling global society what kinds of institutional changes are implied? The purposive pursuit of nonkilling conditions of global life portends institutional changes as pervasive in scope to those associated with the global diffusion of contemporary communication and information technologies. A nonkilling perspective may be absorbed or integrated in old structures, such as in efforts to integrate participatory democracy, gender, race, class, and environmental concerns across political science specialties. Or it may lead to restructuring the old, to establishment of parallel transitional institutions, or to creation of completely new or hybrid institutions combining every source of strength for full-force pursuit of nonkilling transformation.

To take seriously the attainability of nonkilling societies implies need for institutions devoted to nonkilling scientific and humanist discovery, to education and training for nonviolence, to life-affirming problem-solving, to nonkilling security, and to creation of services for nonviolent well-being in every sector of society.

Just as democracies are made by democrats who understand what they are, know how to make them work, and are motivated to make them work—nonkilling societies and institutions will be made by nonkilling individuals. So will nonkilling political science. There are many paths to nonkilling awakening and none can be prescribed for all. Birth, faith, intellect, trauma, compassion, cost-benefit analysis, simulation, and meditation are all paths to nonkilling discovery and action.

The vast historical and contemporary evidence of human capacity to make nonkilling commitments should encourage each of us to discover our own transformational capabilities.

A Nonkilling Department of Political Science

Whereas a nonkilling spirit needs to be infused in each existing political science specialization, department, and association—a new nonkilling department can be envisioned as a prototype for restructuring present ones, and for creation of new departments in emerging world universities.

The department departs from a sense of common purpose: to eliminate killing, threats to kill, and their lethal correlates from global life. This distinguishes it from departments favoring liberal democracy based on violence, scientific socialism based on violence, or authoritarian order based on violence. The nonkilling department is no more value-laden. It is just a different value.

Assuming the present progression of learning from introductory courses to doctoral studies, the department explicitly seeks to nurture character and skills needed for realizing and maintaining nonkilling societies. Four skills are fundamental: for research, for education and training, for action, and for critical reflection expressed through the media of communication and in everyday life.

Entering students are vividly confronted with the lethal legacy of human history and invited to take up the challenge of removing killing from the human condition, as professional political scientists or citizen servant leaders,. They are then empowered with understanding of human capacity for creativity (Boorstin 1983; 1992; 1998), for political innovation (Finer 1997), and for lives of peaceful service to advance human dignity in every area of social life (Josephson 1985).

A next step is to review major contemporary challenges to problem-solving engagement (violence, economy, human rights, environment, cooperation), contemporary political institutions and problem-solving processes (local, national, international, global), and most recent knowledge related to the logic of nonkilling analysis and principles of action that can contribute to present decisions to realize nonkilling futures.

A further step is to offer students opportunities to explore a set of alternative but related modes of problem-solving engagement and community service that will enable testing and matching of interests and talents. This requires introduction to skills for research, education-training, leader-citizen action, and critical political evaluation. This is not to deny possibilities for multiple interests and competencies. But it is to recognize that all four modes of engagement must be pursued supremely well to facilitate nonviolent social transformation. Recognition and cooperation among mutually supportive competencies that is characteristic of village artisans and championship teams in sports is needed.

With such preparation the next step is to pursue individual or group projects to engage appropriate skills in research, education, action, and critical reflection to create alternatives to physical violence, structural violence, violations of human rights, environmental degradation, and violence-prone antagonisms that inhibit problem-solving cooperation. These projects may be directed to local, national, international, or global conditions. The results of such projects, presented as graduating theses, are contributed to a departmental memory bank and published on the Worldwide Web to assist individual and societal decision-making.

Graduates proceed to innovative careers in public service and civil society (see related institutions below). They may seek advanced training in correlated M.A. and Ph.D. programs in nonkilling political science, enter existing fields or create new fields of political science inquiry (Appendices B, C), or carry forward interests into other disciplines and vocations.

The nonkilling department is explicitly service- and vocationally-oriented. It features cumulative advancement of knowledge and skills from introductory to advanced doctoral studies. Faculty and degree candidates form innovative enclaves across levels around shared interests in applying modes of engagement to specific problem-solving needs. The department explicitly seeks to facilitate mutually supportive relationships between discovery of new knowledge, its use in education and training, and its application in societal problem-solving. In its own discourse and modes of resolving conflict it seeks progressively to exemplify characteristics of a nonkilling society. A culture of co-gender partnership between men and women on the basis of equality, the heart of a nonkilling society, is celebrated and respected. Provisions are made for career-long periodic feedback from graduates to identify new needs for research and to advise on more adequate preparation of students for coping with unforeseen tasks. Experienced community leaders and colleagues from other disciplines, sometimes through joint appointments, contribute to collegial creativity. Since nonkilling knowledge and skills are global, the department reaches out to engage collegial talents throughout the world through direct participation and through computerized and other communication systems. The local community is viewed as a functionally equivalent context for confronting problems affecting global well-being.

A University Shanti Sena (Peace Corps)

Transition to nonkilling societies implies creation of a nonviolent student community service corps as an alternative to military training often provided or required in many world colleges and universities. Leadership responsibility may be assumed by a department of political science but members may be drawn from all disciplines.

The Shanti Sena—however named—is a disciplined, distinctively identifiable force whose members are trained for nonviolent conflict resolution and reconciliation, community security and civilian defense, paramedical life-saving, disaster relief, and constructive service in response to community needs. Participation parallels and complements academic work nurturing character and skills of leadership. It draws upon the life-celebrating inspiration of all faiths, the uplifting spirit of music and the arts, the vitality of sports, and the satisfaction of genuine service to others. The Shanti Sena can be called upon to serve in times of crisis on and off campuses and provides a pool of leadership talent for other social institutions. It can be financed and supported in ways no less adequate than those provided contemporary training for military service. It can also be adapted for pre-university education. A valuable source of practical experience for organizing a Shanti Sena in educational institutions is provided by the work of Professor N. Radhakrishnan at Gandhi Rural University in India (Radhakrishnan 1997a; 1997b). To this can be added training principles and practices emerging from the Khudai Khidmatgars (Servants of God), an 80,000-strong nonviolent Muslim liberation army in India during 1930-47 (Banerjee 2000: 73-102), and the Kingian movement for nonviolent social change (LaFayette and Jehnsen 1995; 1996) as well as other nonviolent training experiences (War Resisters League 1989).

Nonkilling Universities

Transition to nonkilling societies implies requirements for knowledge and skills beyond capabilities of any single discipline or university department. Thus the nonkilling transformation of political science means to call upon and respond to the potential contributions of all the social sciences, natural sciences, humanities and professions. It implies need for entire universities devoted to nonkilling service to life in local, national, international, and global communities.

Universities have shown themselves capable of total mobilization of intellectual and human resources for supreme lethality in war. As Harvard University President James B. Conant declared on June 18, 1942, "To speed the day when the Axis powers surrender without conditions, we now dedicate the resources of this ancient society of scholars." Harvard became known as "Conant's Arsenal" as commitment to war-fighting reshaped its institutional life. Young Harvard physics students were recruited to work on the top secret interdisciplinary atomic bomb project at Los Alamos, New Mexico. As one reminisced, "It was a kind of scientific utopia. . . . An open society of the best minds available, freely exchanging ideas without consideration of age, academic rank or previous achievement" (*Harvard Magazine,* September–October 1995: cover; 32, 43).

Should not universities, old and new, take up as vigorously the task of eliminating wars and all forms of lethality that threaten human survival and well-being? The reluctance of universities to introduce "peace studies" courses, programs, or departments—or to include "nonviolence" as a central theme in multimillion dollar-endowed universitywide programs in "ethics" or "values"—provides a basis from which to measure future nonkilling progress in higher education.

Nonkilling Political Parties

Applied nonkilling political science implies services by nonkilling political parties that participate in need-responsive processes of societal problem-solving for the well-being of all. A generic term for such parties might be an *ahimsa sarvodaya* party (*ahimsa,* nonviolence; *sarvodaya,* well-being of all). Such parties to emerge creatively in concept, name, organization, and activities out of specific sociocultural conditions.

The goals of nonkilling parties are to contribute to the realization of nonkilling societies, locally and globally. They differ from past parties in that they are not class-based but seek to aggregate and express the interests of all—for everyone benefits from absence of lethality and its correlates and from the presence of nonkilling conditions of freedom, justice, and material well-being. The presence of several parties, competing on nonkilling principles, can be expected.

The anticipated constructive contribution of nonkilling political parties in electoral competition, public policy-making, and other activities departs from Gandhian prohibitions against direct political participation. Gandhi's last advice to nonviolent constructive workers in December 1947 was to stay out of politics because politics inevitably corrupts (*Collected Works* 90: 223–4). Instead, workers for a nonviolent society should work in civil society among people whose needs are greatest, influencing politicians and policy from outside. Logically this means to let other people become corrupt and make decisions affecting multibillion dollar tax extractions, millions of people, and every aspect of social life—including war, security, food, clothing, housing, health, education, economy, culture, and environment—while nonviolent activists and their people seek to influence the corrupt and their supporters to do good. However, to the credit of Gandhi's foresight he accompanied his nonpolitical admonition with participatory anticipation: "But a stage may come when the people themselves may feel and say that they want us and no one else to wield the power. The question could then be reconsidered" (223).

Nonkilling political parties are logical institutions to help bring about nonkilling social transformation. Naturally conditions favorable for their emergence will differ widely. Nowhere will it be easy, even where parties, elections, and representative bodies are socially accepted. Nonkilling political parties can participate in protracted sacrificial struggles to contribute to processes and policies that respond to the needs of all. To note a few contemporary issues in contention illustrates the challenging task of combining new knowledge, new skills, new forms of organization and new policies in effective problem-solving action. Among them abortion, capital punishment, conscription, war, armed revolution, terrorism, genocide, criminality, social violence, cultural violence, disarmament, and economic demilitarization. Nevertheless progress can be made through creativity, courage, global solidarity, and processes of social learning.

Public Service Departments of Nonviolence

Needed at all levels of governance are public service departments of nonviolence with cabinet responsibilities. Their tasks are to monitor community conditions related to the logic of nonkilling political analysis, to support professional training for prevention and post-lethal transformative rehabilitation, and to advise on public policies that will facilitate nonkilling community well-being. Since conditions of violence pervasively affect the quality of life of a community, public service attention to them merits no less commitment than to garbage disposal or provision of a clean water supply.

A department of nonviolence will aggregate violent statistics and recommendations for violence-eliminating actions from all public and private sources. It will make periodic status reports together with nonkilling policy recommendations to governmental decision-makers and to members of civil society much in the role of an independent auditing agency. Among areas needful of comprehensive oversight are: homicide and suicide; family violence (children, women, spousal, elderly); school violence; workplace violence; criminal and gang violence; police violence; prison violence; media violence; sports violence; economic violence; military-paramilitary-guerrilla violence; and post-lethality traumatic stress effects upon killers, their relatives, relatives of victims, and upon general societal consciousness. The reports should stress strengths and weaknesses of nonviolent transformative capabilities and make recommendations for more effective problem-solving actions. Progress to be reported with no less salience than fluctuations in stock market quotations, sports scores, or the weather.

Nonkilling Common Security Institutions

Transition to nonkilling societies requires nonkilling common security forces, akin to traditional military and police, for protective and humanitarian service operations by land, sea, and air. Such forces to be trained for preventive, crisis coping, and restorative actions—and for after-action evaluations of effectiveness. Leadership may come from conversion of existing military and police academies or from new nonviolent service academies where integrated training can be received by all, followed by branch specialization for specific tasks. The Shanti Sena of universities can be another source of leadership.

The prospect of developing nonviolent common security forces should not be dismissed lightly in view of current trends in some military and police establishments toward violence prevention, engagement in lightly armed peacekeeping operations and humanitarian relief, exploration of usefulness of nonlethal weapons, and receptivity to training in nonviolent methods of conflict resolution.

Nonviolent common security implies engagement of entire populations at local, national, and international levels. This can be facilitated by organization of nonviolence study circles and civic Shanti Sena centered on residences, schools, places of worship, workplaces, and increasingly on electronically networked nonkilling common security communities. Adaptable models for local citizen organization already exist in many fields.

Nonviolent security also implies nonviolent common security councils and nonviolent intelligence agencies at national and transnational levels as well as nonviolent cultural attachés in diplomatic establishments. Nonviolent common security councils are needed to provide policy alternatives for violence-prone nation-states and their lethal allies. A nonviolent global common security council at the United Nations level, for example, can be formed by nations that rank lowest on indicators of lethality: no nuclear weapons, no armies, no capital punishment, low homicide rates, no arms trade, and so forth. Nonviolent intelligence agencies are needed, in conjunction with investigative mass media of communication and citizen alerts, to reveal all forms and threats of lethality and to identify capabilities for countervailing public and private transformational action. Nonviolence specialists in diplomatic establishments are needed no less than conventional military attachés or officers responsible for economic relations. Nonviolence cultural attachés seek to build bridges of discovery, mutual learning, and cooperation between all sources of nonviolent well-being in home and host countries. Global Internet capabilities promise worldwide citizen sharing of common security information with potential for producing concerted nonviolent actions that are not dependent upon conventional governmental, corporate, or media definitions of the situation.

Enhancement of skills for nonkilling public service in governmental and private organizations calls for appropriate institutions for nonviolence training. Perhaps initially as subcomponents and eventually as functionally equivalent replacements, nonviolence training institutions are needed as alternatives to war colleges, national defense universities, military service academies, police academies, and schools of public administration as well as to other violence-accepting professional training schools in civil society.

Nonkilling Civil Society Institutions

Civil society opportunities for contributing to the emergence, maintenance, and creativity of nonkilling societies are potentially infinite. Many nonkilling-oriented institutions already have appeared and others of special significance can be envisioned.

Nonkilling spiritual councils. At each level or for each concentric ring of society, nonkilling spiritual councils are needed to affirm unambiguous respect for life in all matters from birth to death. Such interfaith councils to be composed of religious and humanist exponents of every contextually relevant faith and philosophy who are courageously capable of proclaiming and combining powerful nonkilling truths of their traditions. Such councils, as alternatives to conventional religious and secular apologists for violence, provide inspirational support for all efforts, public and private—local, national, and global—to remove lethality from the human condition. By drawing upon every source of inspiration, nonkilling spiritual councils can become important contributors to strengthening the nonkilling conscience of humankind by evoking capabilities inherent in every individual and social institution.

Nonkilling consulting groups. Drawing upon global resources, nonkilling consulting and advisory groups are needed to assist identification of problem-solving alternatives within and across societies. Combining task-specific spiritual, scientific, skill, organizational, and other resources, such groups, directly or indirectly, make themselves available to help all who seek to prevent bloodshed, stop ongoing slaughter, and create conditions of stable reconciliation and reconstruction. The operations of such nonkilling consulting teams differ from those of conventional negotiators backed by threat of lethal force or economic sanctions—or those of single voices of moral suasion—by their combination of unequivocal commitment to nonkilling, multiple competencies, and independence from control by violent states and their lethal antagonists. Privately financed institutions capable of providing such consulting services, aggregating their experiences, and improving their effectiveness are needed. Quaker conflict resolution and humanitarian services, as well as those of other religious and humanitarian relief agencies, provide pioneering partial prototypes of what is needed.

Transnational problem-solving consortia. Complementing what may be termed "top down" nonkilling political institutions (for example, parties, public service departments, and common security institutions), "bottom-up" consortia of powerful nonkilling transformational forces are needed. An example is the Unrepresented Nations and Peoples Organization (UNPO), a coalition of peoples with distinctive identities explicitly committed to nonviolent action to influence the United Nations, governments, and other institutions to recognize their collective human rights. Amnesty International, Greenpeace, and the International Fellowship of Reconciliation provide other examples. Participants in nonkilling consortia need not agree on all positions advocated by members except upon removal of killing from the global condition. Such consortia need to be developed within and across zones in the funnel of killing and in the major problem-solving areas of violence, economics, human rights, environment, and cooperation. Eventually a powerful global citizens consortium for a nonkilling world, a partnership of women and men, should emerge as a force for universal well-being.

Nonkilling training institutions. As consciousness about pervasive threats of violence and needs for constructive nonviolent alternatives intensify, there are increasing demands for training in skills of nonviolent leadership for conflict resolution and nonviolent social change. Skilled trainers are in great demand from the Kingian, Gandhian, Buddhist, Christian, and secular nonviolent traditions. Needs range from those of citizens movements on every social justice issue to those of institutions such as schools, workplaces, police, and prisons. Civil society institutions are needed to provide nonviolent citizen training as with any other skill, and to train and certify professional trainers.

Nonkilling leadership study and revitalization centers. Institutions are needed to which leaders of nonviolent organizations and movements can come for periods of revitalization, reflection, writing, and sharing of experiences. Often periods of imprisonment or hospitalization are the only pauses for leaders engaged in life-threatening, stressful commitments to bring about nonviolent social change. A voluntary nonviolent functional equivalent is needed. Where leaders have been tortured, cooperation with centers for rehabilitation of victims of torture is essential. Dispersed throughout the world, centers for nonviolent leadership can provide opportunities for spiritual and physical revitalization, autobiographical reflection and biographical study, dialogues with experienced colleagues similarly committed to nonkilling principles from various countries, and foresightful contemplation of next steps forward. These centers may be privately endowed as independent institutions or adopted by host institutions committed to nonkilling social transformation.

Centers for nonkilling creativity in the arts. Institutions are needed for encouragement of nonkilling creativity within and across the arts. As the Swiss writer Romain Rolland quotes Tolstoy, "Art must suppress violence, and only art can do so" (Rolland 1911: 203). In a study of nonviolence in the poetry of Shelley, Art Young observes, "Nonviolence is more than a system of political thought; it is the stuff of poetry and of life" (1975: 165). Reminiscent of the importance of martial music for military morale, a maxim in the Kingian tradition maintains, "If you don't have a song, you don't have a movement" (Young 1996: 161–184).

One institutional model—patterned after private centers that sponsor creative communities among the seven arts or among painters, poets, and writers—is to provide opportunities for artists of every inspiration to come together to celebrate transformative nonkilling creativity in response to human lethality. Among arts to which the challenge of nonkilling creativity can be addressed are literature, poetry, painting, sculpture, music, dance, theater, film, television, photography, architecture, clothing design, and commercial arts of the mass media. To find ways out of violence challenges all the arts. An alternative to conventional murder mysteries, for example, can be to create nonviolent detectives who prevent by skillful means murders and suicides *before* they occur. Synergistic nonkilling creativity among the arts can uplift the human spirit and imagination for the crucial transformational tasks ahead.

For global recognition, benefactors should establish awards for nonkilling contributions to the arts no less significant than encouragement provided by the various Nobel prizes.

Nonkilling research and policy analysis institutes. Just as private institutes are established to advise governments and the general public on matters ranging from international security policies to all matters of political, economic, social, and cultural life, nonkilling policy institutes are needed to provide information and analysis to assist societal decision-making. They can amplify the problem-solving commitments of nonkilling political science in the fields of violence, economy, human rights, environment, and cooperation. They can support the applied efforts of nonkilling spiritual councils, parties, common security institutions, consulting groups, and other civil society institutions as well as provide information needed by individual citizens.

Nonkilling media of communication. Nonkilling media of communication are needed to provide information, news and commentary to assist individual and public policy decision-making. This does not mean media that overlook human capacities for killing but that go beyond conventional media messages that killing is inevitable, often laudable, and entertaining. The editorial decisions of nonkilling media in the transitional era can reflect the logic of nonkilling political analysis. That is, the messages probe deep into the realities of violence; bring to consciousness countervailing nonviolent realities; report on transformational processes, successes and set-backs; and give voice to creative nonkilling aspirations in all arts, sciences, humanities, professions, and vocations of everyday life. This approach is no more value-laden than media that fail to challenge the assumption of perpetual lethality and incessantly contribute, explicitly or implicitly, to keeping the mind locked in violent pessimism. Media alternatives are needed in newspapers and magazines, on the radio and television, in films, and on global computerized information networks. Nonkilling political scientists can be one source of commentary and analysis.

Nonkilling memorials. To recover and celebrate the nonkilling heritage of civilization, memorials to individuals, groups, organizations, unknown heroes and heroines, and events need to be constructed respectfully in every society. To be celebrated are all those who have refused to kill and have contributed to the long march toward nonkilling global civilization. This is not to remove the statues and memorials to the triumphant and defeated killers of history that dot the planet—since they recall the realities of historical lethality. But nonkilling memorials are needed to remind us that there have always been proponents of nonviolent alternatives that are now increasingly imperative for human survival. Among those to be celebrated are religious figures, martyrs who spoke truth to violent power, war resisters, conscientious objectors, opponents of the death penalty, poets of peace, and the unsung masses of women and men who resisted injustices without violence at the risk of imprisonment, torture, and death.

Nonkilling zones of peace. Implied civil society institutions are nonkilling zones of peace ranging from organizations through rural and urban communities to national and international agreements. Harbingers are religious sanctuaries, zones of peace declared by villages victimized between armed revolutionary and counterrevolutionary forces, expandable cease fire areas, movements for weapons-free societies, citizen efforts to reclaim residential areas from criminal and gang violence, and international treaties to establish nuclear-weapons-free zones. The identification of, networking among, and introduction of supportive nonkilling institutions into such varied zones of peace for mutual support and diffusion is a major nonkilling institutional development challenge.

Nonkilling economic enterprises. If the enterprises of war and cultures of violence are said to be profitable for some even if unspeakably costly for many, enterprises for nonkilling well-being should become even more profitable for all. Viewed from a nonkilling perspective and from the perspective of anticipated growing demand for nonviolent material and cultural goods, services, entertainment, and recreational alternatives, the opportunities for nonkilling entrepreneurship are limitless. One way to begin to identify alternatives is to inventory violence-serving enterprises and envision their nonkilling opposites. For war toys substitute peace toys, for video game lethality substitute exciting nonviolent ingenuity, for the armaments industry substitute the disarmament industry, for violent media entertainment offer dramatic creations of nonkilling arts, and for labor to destroy substitute work to improve the quality of life. Experience is provided by examples of nonviolent economic conversion that accompany periods of demilitarization. But beyond simple economic reversal is to seek to identify the genuine needs of people in transition to nonkilling societies in their global context and to create services capable of responding to them.

Centers for global nonkilling. The vision of a nonkilling world implies institutions capable of facilitating transition from completely holistic perspectives. Such institutions must be firmly rooted in the nonkilling commonalities of world spiritual and cultural traditions and must become capable of creative catalysis of global scientific, skill, artistic, and institutional resources to assist humankind to perceive paths of nonviolent liberation from lethality and its consequences. In contemporary computer terms such centers should be creative catalysts of nonviolent "software" that can serve human needs through the "hardware" services of government and institutions of civil society. To be effective such centers should be maximally independent from violence-demanding governments and from control by exclusionary private interests. They should be substantially endowed in perpetuity by visionary benefactors, mass subscriptions, and other means.

A center for global nonkilling takes as its goal discovery and elicitation of utmost human creativity in areas such as the following: nonviolence in spiritual and philosophical traditions; bio-neuroscience and nonviolence; gender relations and nonviolence; economics and nonviolence; communications and nonviolence; science, technology and nonviolence; nonviolence and the environment; the vocations and nonviolence; education and nonviolence; nonviolence and the arts; nonviolence and sports; the role of the military and police in nonviolent change; nonviolent leadership; and nonviolent human futures.

A major contextual and historical task is to inventory nonviolent global cultural resources based upon locally-centered inquiry in every country and region. This requires inquiry into nonkilling historical traditions, present manifestations, and future prospects. Aggregated on a global scale, such discoveries will provide humanity with our first comprehensive understanding of nonkilling human capabilities from which future progress can be measured.

Centers for global nonkilling should be equipped with a global situation room in which the ongoing realities of killing, threats to kill, and related deprivations, can be vividly juxtaposed against countervailing nonkilling transformational resources available to humankind. Constantly confronting the challenges of lethality, such centers, drawing upon creative advances in knowledge as above, can suggest combinations of spiritual, scientific, skill, artistic, and institutional resources to assist transformational public policy, research, education, and training by all who seek the survival and well-being of humankind.

Needed Nonkilling Institutions

A political science committed to tasks of realizing nonkilling societies will educate and innovate for action through appropriate institutions, beginning with itself. Institutions are needed for life-respecting spiritual affirmation. For discovery, integration, and sharing of knowledge. For public policy decision-making. For nonviolent common security. For economic well-being. And for celebrating life in all the arts and vocations.

The tasks of transition call for creatively integrative centers for global nonkilling—committed to understanding and facilitating responsiveness to nonkilling needs of all. The strength of nonkilling institutions derives from mutually supportive individuals. Every political scientist and each person can be *a center* for global nonkilling to facilitate transition to a nonkilling world.

Chapter 6

NONKILLING GLOBAL POLITICAL SCIENCE

> We are in a new era. The old methods and solutions no longer suffice. We must have new thoughts, new ideas, new concepts . . . . We must break out of the strait-jacket of the past.
>
> General Douglas MacArthur

> Someone has to have sense enough and even strategy to cut off the chains of violence and destruction in history.
>
> Martin Luther King, Jr.

> Certainly all historical experience confirms the truth—that man would not have attained the possible unless time and time again he had reached out for the impossible.
>
> Max Weber

> We are daily witnessing the phenomenon of the impossible of yesterday becoming the possible of today.
>
> Mohandas K. Gandhi

Toward Liberation From Lethality

The time has come to set forth human killing as a problem to be solved rather than to accept enslavement by it as a condition to be endured forever. The deliberate killing of human beings, one by one, mass by mass, and the many by machines, has reached a stage of pathological self-destruction. Killing that has been expected to liberate, protect, and enrich has become instead a source of insecurity, impoverishment, and threat to human and planetary survival. Humanity is suffering from what Craig Comstock has termed the "pathology of defense" when that which is intended to defend becomes itself the source of self-destruction (Comstock 1971). Defensive guns in the home kill family members, bodyguards kill their own heads of state, armies violate and impoverish their own peoples, nuclear weapons proliferate to threaten their inventors and possessors. A Nonkilling Declaration of Independence from violence within ourselves and our societies is needed.

The pursuit of human aspirations by violence in the modern era has resulted in incalculable bloodshed, material deprivation, and psychological traumas reverberating across generations. The hopes of humanity in the past two centuries have been emblazoned on banners bequeathed by the French Revolution—"liberté, égalité, fraternité." Killing for freedom has been the legacy of the American revolution. Killing for equality has been the legacy of the Russian and Chinese revolutions. Killing for peace has been the heritage of two centuries of war, revolution, and counterrevolution. The lesson to be learned is that true freedom, equality, and the fraternity-sorority of peace cannot be realized without fundamental uprooting of the legacy of lethality. The mountains of massacred who have been sacrificed for good and evil cry out for us to learn this lesson.

This means to challenge and change the assumption of the emerging world academic discipline of political science that killing is inevitable and good for the well-being of humankind. It means to question and overturn one of the most powerful tenets of ancient wisdom and contemporary political belief. An analogue can be found in the overthrow of the theory of "laudable pus" in the history of medicine. For some seventeen centuries the teaching of the immensely authoritative Greek physician Galen (c.130-c.200) prevailed that the pus formed around a wound was nature's way of restoring health. This was challenged in 1867 by Lister in his seminal *Lancet* paper, "On the Antiseptic Principle in the Practice of Surgery," that led not without controversy to the invention and adoption of antiseptics (Ackerknecht 1982: 77; Garrison 1929: 116; 589–90). The belief that killing is natural and functionally healthy for politics is the "laudable pus theory" of political science.

If political scientists, scholars who dedicate their lives to the study of political power in its multi-faceted manifestations from family life to world war, do not challenge seriously the assumption of lethality, then why should we expect political leaders and citizens of the world to do so? Yet throughout history and increasingly in the present era leaders and citizens unaided by political science emerge who explicitly seek to realize conditions of freedom, equality, and peace by principled nonkilling means. An example is the "burning of weapons" by 7,000 pacifist peasant Doukhobors resisting military conscription in Russia in 1895 (Tarasoff 1995: 8–10). There is a manifest gap between lethality-accepting political science, and pioneers of lethality-rejecting politics. In the twentieth century the legacies of Tolstoy, Gandhi, Abdul Ghaffar Khan, Martin Luther King, Jr., and Petra Kelly—courageously carried forward by leaders such as the Dalai Lama, Aung San Suu Kyi, and Desmond Tutu—inspired and supported by unsung heroines and heroes who make nonviolent servant leadership possible—are harbingers of powerful nonkilling politics of the future.

Are political scientists belatedly to follow nonkilling sacrificial successes by individuals and popular movements, after clinging to the violence-accepting status quo—like cautious beneficiaries of authoritarian regimes who hang on until disaffected demonstrations sweep them aside? Are political scientists then to join in nonkilling democratic celebrations? Or is political science after the manner of medical science to dedicate itself to diagnosis of the pathology of lethality, and to discovery of prescriptions and treatments that can be shared with all who seek to remove killing from global life?

Thesis of Nonkilling Capabilities

The thesis presented here is that a nonkilling global society is possible and that changes in the academic discipline of political science and its social role can help to bring it about. The case for the realizability of nonkilling societies rests upon at least seven grounds. Most humans do not kill. Powerful nonkilling potential resides in the spiritual heritage of humankind. Science demonstrates and forecasts nonkilling human capabilities. Transitional nonkilling public policies such as abolition of the death penalty and recognition of conscientious objection to military service have been adopted by even violence-created nation states. Various social institutions based upon nonkilling principles exist that in combination already constitute functional equivalents of nonkilling societies. Nonviolent popular struggles for political and socioeconomic change demonstrate an increasingly powerful alternative to revolutionary lethality. Roots of nonkilling inspiration and experience can be discovered in historical traditions throughout the world. Ultimately the promise of nonkilling transition rests upon examples of nonkilling individuals, men and women, celebrated and unknown, whose courageous lives testify to its achievability.

Implications for Political Science

It is accepted that humans, biologically and by conditioning are capable of both killing and nonkilling. But it is observed that most humans have not been killers and that a range of social institutions based upon nonkilling principles already have been created that can serve as prototype components of nonkilling societies. Furthermore, present and expectable scientific advances promise knowledge for removing causes of killing, for strengthening causes of nonkilling, and for bringing about conditions of nonkilling societies. Given these observations, the acceptance of inescapable lethality as an assumption upon which to base the academic discipline and social role of political science is at the very least problematical. Therefore to question the assumption of killing and its implications throughout what might be called the "deadly discipline" of political science—among others—is appropriate. Political science, along with other disciplines and vocations, must recover nonviolent experiences of the past, recognize present nonviolent capabilities, project nonviolent potentials for the future, and cooperate in advancing this knowledge in research, teaching, and public service for nonkilling social transformation.

The principal elements that need to be combined for nonkilling transformation are clear. *Spirit* (S_1), profound commitments not to kill derived from each and all faiths and philosophies. *Science* (S_2), knowledge from all the arts, sciences, and professions that bear upon the causes of killing and nonkilling transformation. *Skills* (S_3), individual and group methods for expressing spirit and science in transformative action. *Song* (S_4), the inspiration of music and all the arts, making the science and practice of nonkilling politics neither dismal nor deadly but a powerful celebration of life. To combine, develop and amplify these four elements in effective service, democratic *Leadership* (L), *Citizen Competence* (C), implementing *Institutions* (I) and supporting *Resources* (R) are necessary.

This combination of elements can be summarized as:

S^4 x L C I R = Nonkilling Global Transformation

Spirit, science, skills, and song, creatively combined through need-responsive processes of democratic leadership and citizen empowerment, amplified by institutional expressions and resource commitments can contribute to realization of a nonkilling world.

Theory and Research

The horror of human lethality calls for political science inquiry into a four-part logic of political analysis that can provide knowledge necessary to prevent convergence of forces that result in killings from homicide to genocide and nuclear annihilation of cities to potential extinction of planetary life. In political science consciousness, killing must move from the violence-accepting periphery to the center of analytical and problem-solving attention. This means concentrated effort to understand the causes of killing; the causes of nonkilling; the causes of transition from killing to nonkilling and vice versa; and the characteristics of completely killing-free societies. Such knowledge is needed to assist identification of nonkilling alternatives and transformative actions within and across the converging zones of the funnel of lethality: neuro-biological, structural, cultural, socialization, and killing zones.

Education and Training

To carry forward such knowledge-seeking and transformative tasks implies prerequisites in the education and training of political scientists, in the structure of curricula, in the organization of academic political science departments, in relations with other disciplines, and in the research-education-action role of political science in society.

The overall goal of political science education and training becomes to nurture creativity for and skill in nonkilling problem-solving. Some guiding principles are to review the legacy of creative lives and institutions; to assist exploration of individual interests and skills; to seek cumulative knowledge and skill development; to engage in self-selected problem-solving projects; to provide for parallel constructive community service; and to orient toward and support nonkilling political science vocations.

After vivid introduction to the horrifying history of lethality and the inspiring legacy of nonkilling creativity, the curriculum presents the logic of nonkilling political analysis and challenges engagement in discovery of principles and processes for effective problem-solving action. Participants review the causes of killing, nonkilling, transitions, and hypotheses about the characteristics of nonkilling societies. From this perspective, historical developments of political institutions and processes, locally and globally, are examined. Problem-solving challenges are posed—such as homicide, democide, genocide, and disarmament; economic lethality; human rights atrocities; ecological biocide; and destructive divisiveness versus cooperation across diversity. Opportunities to develop skills in modes of problem-solving engagement are offered: research, teaching, servant leadership, and critical communication. On these foundations individual and group projects to solve problems and develop skills are pursued and presented. A parallel university-wide Shanti Sena (Peace Corps) provides complementary leadership training for disciplined community service.

Graduates proceed to meet needs for researchers, educators, leaders, and communicators in transitional public and private institutions. They respond to social needs for creative problem-solving service. Post-graduate training provides advanced preparation for service in politics, government, and civil society to meet increasing contemporary needs for skills in violence prevention and nonviolent social change. Problem-solving engagements parallel those in undergraduate education. Working groups are formed to advance skills in research, education, action, and reflection to solve problems of violence, economy, human rights, environment, cooperation, and other issues. Masters degree and doctoral candidates serve with faculty as guides, mentors, and co-learners in undergraduate projects.

Nonkilling political science implies high aspirations in doctoral training to prepare professionals who are creators themselves and skilled in facilitating the creativity of others. Not all can be expected to master every needed skill, but all can share understanding of required tasks, seek creative contributions to the maximum extent of competence, and learn how to support the problem-solving contributions of others both within and without the academic community.

Doctoral training will require intensive study of the foundations of nonkilling political science; understanding of local and global problem-solving needs; preparation in skills of nonkilling scholarly leadership; understanding of qualitative and quantitative modes of inquiry (including languages); mastery of research methods essential for tasks at hand; and engagement in advanced projects. The latter to encompass discovery of new knowledge and application of existing knowledge to improve education and training, institutional development, and processes of problem-solving.

Nonkilling scholarly leadership requires preparation for versatile performance of needed social roles. Fundamental is an opportunity for autobiographical reflection on origins of beliefs and attitudes toward killing and nonkilling. Preparation is needed for teaching to facilitate student creativity. For departmental leadership to facilitate collegial creativity. For cross-disciplinary cooperation. For consultancy to facilitate nonkilling change in state and civil society. For critically constructive media communications. And for direct nonviolent servant leadership (Greenleaf 1977).

In its own social relationships a nonkilling department of political science must seek to express through trial and error the desired characteristics of a nonkilling society. This means to affirm nonsectarian but multi-faith spiritual and humanist respect for life. To engender responsibility for the well-being of all. To improve need-responsive, participatory processes of decision-making. To celebrate diversity and dignity of all. To experiment with co-gender and distributed leadership functions. To be prepared to call upon nonviolent problem-solving consultants at times of seemingly intractable conflict. To be open to the contributions of other disciplines and professions. To encourage innovative enclaves to solve scientific problems. And to recognize that a nonkilling global society is rooted in individuals and the local community.

Long-term mutual consulting relationships should be established with graduates who proceed to work in the fields of research, education, leadership, communications, and other areas of social life. Their experiences can greatly assist identifying research needs, improving preparation in needed skills, and evoking creativity to overcome obstacles to nonkilling transformation. However diverse in other respects, all who accept the challenge of nonkilling political science can join together in sustained, mutual assistance.

Problem-Solving

Nonkilling political science implies combination of basic and applied science in explicit problem-solving engagement. Problems will vary as defined in contexts of complex social change. Five problems of critical importance are globally salient: violence and disarmament, economic holocaust, human rights atrocities, environmental degradation, and failures of problem-solving cooperation. All related and exacerbated directly and indirectly by readiness to kill. A contemporary slogan holds that there will be "no peace without justice"—implying that violence and war will continue or be necessary to protest or change unjust conditions. But from a nonkilling perspective there will be "no justice without nonkilling." For killing and threats to kill have contributed to the creation and maintenance of injustice. In the case of unequal treatment of women, for example, as Petra Kelly has observed: "The unfair sexual distribution of power, resources, and responsibilities is legitimized by ancient traditions, enshrined in law, and enforced when necessary by male violence" (Kelly 1994: 15).

Engagement in problem-solving does not imply that nonkilling political science is omniscient or the source of every solution. But it does imply that application of knowledge derived from nonkilling political analysis and from principles and practices of nonviolent action can improve processes of social decision-making that are responsive to the needs of all. In this sense it promises a nonviolent contribution to advancement beyond the violence-based democratic tradition (Goldman 1990).

Institutions

The knowledge-seeking, education-training, and problem-solving objectives of nonkilling political science imply needs for implementational institutions. These range from new or restructured political science departments, even entire universities (including global communication equivalents that combine talents imbedded in or outside existing institutions), to nonmilitary Shanti Sena training units, nonkilling public policy institutions, nonkilling common security forces, nonkilling political parties, and nonkilling institutional innovations in every sector of civil society. The creation of and service in such institutions, as well as in transformation of existing institutions to remove lethality from local and global life, offer vocations of utmost creativity for all who study and practice the science of nonkilling politics.

Obstacles and Inspirations

At the dawn of the twenty-first century political science is challenged to take up the task of contributing to the realization of a nonkilling global society. It is not only desirable, but imperative. Political scientists cannot evade this responsibility by objecting to value-bias and claiming "realistic" scientific neutrality that in truth translates into readiness to kill. Such neutrality has never been true. If it were, political scientists would not care whether the society or world in which they lived was free or unfree, just or unjust, affluent or impoverished, at peace or at war, victorious or defeated. They would find joy in teaching their students that political scientists have no value preferences and therefore do not shape their research, teaching, and public service projects to favor some over others. For them there would be no choice between Hitler's holocaust and Gandhi's satyagraha.

Political scientists also cannot avoid the task of creating a nonkilling political science simply on grounds that other values such as freedom, equality, or security are more important than nonkilling. Nonkilling is at least of equal importance because humanity has arrived at a condition where all of these values are threatened without a powerful commitment to a nonkilling ethic in political science and political life. Materialism and morality have arrived at the same conclusion. If tradition has taught that we must kill to be free, equal, and secure—the present teaches that unless we stop killing not only freedom and equality are in jeopardy but our very survival—individual, social, and ecological—is imperiled. We have reached a point where the science and practice of politics must be aligned with the life-supporting forces of society and nature. It is not only good morality, and good practicality, but it is also this era's imperative for good political science.

In the process of transition, of course, opposition can be expected from forces of thought and action that derive identities and perceived benefits from continuation of lethality. Among them are the violent forces of states, their lethal antagonists, and the political, economic, and psychological beneficiaries of cultures of killing. Among these are some but decidedly not all veterans of wars and revolts, their descendants, and others who vicariously derive identity and pride from socially validated celebrations of righteous lethality. Paying homage in martyr cemeteries we are conditioned against sympathy for the enemy dead, fail to see both as victims of political failure, and depart with exhortations to be forever prepared for similar sacrifice, rather than to commit ourselves to ensure that such killing will never happen again.

But among inspiring sources of support for transition to nonkilling political science are experienced admonitions by some of the world's most honored military leaders. Consider the appeal for the abolition of war as matter of imperative "scientific realism" made by General Douglas MacArthur in a speech to the American Legion in 1955:

> You will say at once that although the abolition of war has been the dream of man for centuries, every proposition to that end has been promptly discarded as impossible and fantastic. Every cynic, every pessimist, every adventurer, every swashbuckler in the world has always disclaimed its feasibility. But that was before the science of the past decade made mass destruction a reality. The argument then was along spiritual and moral grounds, and lost . . . . But now the tremendous and present evolution of nuclear and other potentials of destruction has suddenly taken the problem away from its primary consideration as a moral and spiritual question and brought it abreast of scientific realism. It is no longer an ethical question to be pondered solely by learned philosophers and ecclesiastics but a hard core one for the decision of the masses whose survival is at stake . . . . The leaders are the laggards . . . . Never do they state the bald truth, that the next great advance in civilization cannot take place until war is abolished . . . . When will some great figure in power have sufficient imagination to translate this universal wish—which is rapidly becoming a universal necessity—into actuality? We are in a new era. The old methods and solutions no longer suffice. We must have new thoughts, new ideas, new concepts . . . . We must break out of the strait-jacket of the past (Cousins 1987: 67-9).

New nonviolent transformations of the slogans of the French Revolution can be heard in the warnings of General later United States President Dwight D. Eisenhower on the harmful influences of continued violent militarization upon liberty, equality, and fraternity. On *liberty*: "In the councils of government, we must guard against the acquisition of undue influence, whether sought or unsought, by the military industrial complex. We must never let the weight of this combination endanger our liberties or democratic processes. We should take nothing for granted" (Farewell Address, January 17, 1961). On *economic equality*: "Every gun that is made, every warship launched, every rocket fired signifies, in the final sense, a theft from those who hunger and are not fed, those who are cold and not clothed" (Speech to American Society of Newspaper Editors, April 16, 1953). On *fraternity*: "Indeed, I think that people want peace so much that one of these days governments had better get out of their way and let them have it" (BBC TV interview, August 31, 1959).

On December 4, 1996, speaking before the National Press Club in Washington, D.C., the retired former commander of all United States nuclear-war-fighting forces General George Lee Butler called for the complete abolition—not mere reduction—of nuclear weapons and for the United States as their inventor and first user to lead in abolishing them. Otherwise, he cautioned, the United States has no moral authority to prevent other countries from acquiring them. His reasons: "Nuclear weapons are inherently dangerous, hugely expensive, militarily inefficient, and morally indefensible." Thus the General arrived at the long-held conclusion of spiritually motivated Americans such as members of the Swords into Plowshares movement whose opposition to nuclear weapons continues to evoke punishment by confinement in federal prisons. The logic of the nuclear abolitionist movement can be applied to other tools for killing as well.

If these generals, experts in the profession of killing, can raise such profound questions about the continued assumptions of their vocation and its relation to society, cannot political scientists question the violence-accepting presuppositions of their own profession and social role and strive for the global realization of nonkilling societies?

Perhaps most American political scientists and those international colleagues who are adopting components of contemporary American political science are unaware of the nonkilling motivation that contributed to the creation of political science as an academic discipline in the United States. One of its origins was a battlefield vow made in 1863 by a young Union soldier, John W. Burgess, assigned to night sentinel duty after a bloody, daylong battle with Confederate forces in west Tennessee:

> It was still raining in torrents; the lightning shot its wicked tongues athwart the inky sky, and the thunder rolled and reverberated like salvos of heavy artillery through the heavens. With this din and uproar of nature were mingled the cries of wounded and dying animals and the shrieks and groans of wounded and dying men. It was a night of terror to the most hardened soldiers. To one so young and sensitive as myself it was awful beyond description, and it has been a hideous nightmare to this day. It was, however, in the midst of this frightful experience that the first suggestion of my life's work came to me. As I strained my eyes to peer into the darkness and my ears to perceive the first sounds of an approaching enemy, I found myself murmuring to myself: "Is it not possible for man, a being of reason created in the image of God, to solve the problems of his existence by the power of reason and without recourse to the destructive means of physical violence?" And I then registered a vow in heaven that if a kind Providence would deliver me alive from the perils of the existing war, I would devote my life to live by reason and compromise instead of by bloodshed and destruction (Burgess 1934: 28).

Carrying forward his vow, Burgess went on to graduate study in Germany and returned to found the School of Political Science at Columbia College in New York in 1880.

Professor Burgess's subsequent experience forecasts obstacles that contributors to nonkilling political science can expect to confront. These obstacles will vary from minor to extreme severity according to context, and will require courage and global cooperation to overcome them. With his understanding of Germans as fellow human beings, Burgess opposed United States entry into World War I. For him, on the day of entry, August 6, 1917, "with one grievous blow . . . my life's work [was] brought down in irretrievable ruin around me." Amidst the patriotic anti-German war, he lamented that "to be a man of peace and reason today is regarded by the people of the world as tantamount to being a traitor and a coward" (29). Thus Professor Burgess suffered the agony of peacemakers throughout the ages who, perceiving the virtues and faults of antagonists, tend to be condemned by each contender, sometimes at the cost of their lives.

Nonkilling political science no less than nonkilling politics needs to be guided by Gandhi's call to be "truthful, gentle, and fearless" inspired by profound spiritual and humanist respect for life. It will take courage. Amidst global bloodshed, political scientists need be no less committed to life-respecting principles than the peasants of the Sociedad Civil Las Abejas (The Bees Civil Society) formed in 1992 in the Chiapas region of Mexico. The Bees nonviolently strive for justice amidst armed Zapatista rebellion and repressive ruling atrocities. They share Zapastista grievances but avow: "Our way is different. We believe in the Word of God. We know how to read the Bible. We must love our enemy; we cannot kill. Above all, we are poor peasants, brothers and sisters . . . . We are not afraid to die. We are ready to die, but not to kill" (*Peace News,* July 1998: 13, 14).

Why should we expect principled commitments to nonkilling always to come from the "bottom up"—such as from colonized Indians under British imperial domination, from African-Americans under white racist repression, or from poor Mexican peasants? Why not also from the "top down" by local, national, international and global elites, including academic political scientists?

As inquiry into nonkilling capabilities reveals, there are grounds for confidence that humans can bring about nonkilling global transformation. Virtually all component elements of a nonkilling society have been demonstrated somewhere in human experience. It only remains to identify, supplement, and creatively adapt them to local and global needs and conditions. Horrified consciousness of past and present bloodshed can serve as a source of powerful nonkilling motivation and socialization. We must not repeat humanity's murderous mistakes. Therefore we must act to make continuation of killing or reversion to killing impossible.

As reported by anthropologists Clayton and Carole Robarchek (1998), the remarkable ninety percent reduction in homicides by the Waorani people of Ecuador in the short period of thirty years after 1958 shows that humans are capable of rapid nonkilling change. With sixty percent of deaths resulting from homicide over the past century, the Waorani have been considered to be "the most violent society known to anthropology." The homicide rate was 1,000 per 100,000 population as compared with 10 or less per 100,000 for the United States. But in three decades Waorani homicides dropped to 60 per 100,000. The main contributors to change were courageous leadership initiatives by two women Christian missionaries—widow and sister of martyred men who were killed in an unsuccessful attempt to contact the Waorani in 1956; assistance by several Waorani women; introduction of an alternative nonkilling value system; the introduction of new cognitive information including that outsiders were not cannibals, brought back by the Waorani women who had seen the outside world; and the desire of the Waorani themselves to end the endless cycle of fearful vendettas in which whole families are speared to death. Churches were organized and prayerful commitments to stop killing were made. Reduction in homicide was accomplished without police or other coercion and without preceding socioeconomic structural change. On the contrary, structural changes began to follow the combination of new nonkilling spiritual commitment and receipt of new information. Even non-Christian Waorani groups began to change.

For the Robarcheks this remarkable shift in values and structure, though still incomplete, confirms important theoretical assumptions about human behavior:

> People are not considered passive machines pushed into action by ecological, biological, or even sociocultural determinants but active decision-makers picking their ways through fields of options and constraints in pursuit of individually and culturally defined goals in a culturally defined reality that they are continually constructing and reconstructing (1998: 4).

From a nonkilling political science perspective, the Waorani experience provides evidence for the transformational potential inherent in creative leadership for change. What the Waorani can do, political science can do as a profession and in service to society. There is much work to be done, for neither the Waorani nor the world, of course, are killing-free. Incursions by outsiders engaged in energy operations plus raids by Waorani neighbors not yet reached by nonkilling spiritual-cognitive influences have led to some recurrences of bloodshed. Although nonkilling enclaves are possible and essential for global change, the spirit and practice of nonviolence must become universal.

Global Imperative

Nonkilling political science must be global. Global in discovery, creativity, diversity, and effectiveness. Global in spirit, science, skills, song, institutional expressions, and resource commitments. Global in nurturance of creative leadership and empowerment of all to take and support initiatives that celebrate life. Global in compassionate commitment to solve problems in response to human needs. Global in determination to end killing everywhere or no one will be safe anywhere. Global in participation for no discipline, vocation, or society has all the wisdom, skills, and resources required. Global in commitment to local well-being, for in particulars lie the liberating seeds of universals. Global in respect for diversity and in multiple loyalties to the nonkilling well-being of people in one's own and other societies. Global in mutual supportiveness among all who study, teach, and act to end the era of lethality that impedes full realization of liberty, equality, prosperity, and peace. Global as in viewing our planetary home from the moon, conscious of each of us as momentary sparks of life among billions—yet not one insignificant as potential contributors to a nonkilling world.

The goal of ending lethality in global life implies a shift from violence-accepting political science to the science of nonkilling responsiveness to human needs for love, well-being, and free expression of creative potential.

Is a nonkilling society possible?

Is a nonkilling global political science possible?

Yes!

Appendix A

INTERNATIONAL POLITICAL SCIENCE ASSOCIATION NATIONAL ASSOCIATIONS —1999

Name	Year Founded (Predecessor Organization)	Membership
African Association of Political Science	1974 (1973)	1,360
Argentine Association of Political Analysis	1981 (1957)	180
Australasian Political Studies Association	1966 (1952)	425
Austrian Political Science Association	1970 (1951)	537
Flemish Political Science Association	1979 (1951)	450
Association Belge de Science Politique/ Communauté Française de Belgique	1996 (1951)	50
Brazilian Political Science Association	1952	*
Bulgarian Political Science Association	1973 (1968)	72
Canadian Political Science Association	1968 (1913)	1,200
Chilean Political Science Association	*	*
Chinese Association of Political Science	1980	1,025
Croatian Political Science Association	1966	100
Czech Political Science Association	1964	200
Danish Association of Political Science	1960	350
Finnish Political Science Association	1935	550
Association française de science politique	1949	1,030
German Political Science Association	1951	1,300
Hellenic Political Science Association	1957 (1951)	265
Hungarian Political Science Association	1982 (1968)	468
Indian Political Science Association	1935	1,600
Political Studies Association of Ireland	1982	247
Israel Political Science Association	1950	250
Italian Political Science Association		220

Japanese Political Science Association		1,278
Korean Political Science Association	1953	2,000
Korean Association of Social Scientists	1979	1,465
Lithuanian Political Science Association	1991	86
Mexican Political Science Association	*	*
Dutch Political Science Association	1966 (1950)	350
New Zealand Political Studies Association	1974	*
Nigerian Political Science Association	*	*
Norwegian Political Science Association	1956	500
Pakistan Political Science Association	1950	300
Philippine Political Science Association	*	*
Polish Association of Political Science	1950	200
Romanian Association of Political Science	1968	188
Russian Political Science Association	1991 (1960)	300
Slovak Political Science Association	1990	150
Slovenian Political Science Association	1968	220
South African Political Studies Association	1973	186
Spanish Association of Political and Administrative Science	1993 (1958)	253
Swedish Political Science Association	1970	264
Swiss Political Science Association	1950	1,000
Chinese Association of Political Science (Taipei)	1932	350
Political Science Association of Thailand	*	*
Turkish Political Science Association	1964	120
Political Studies Association of the UK	1964	1,200
American Political Science Association	1903	13,300
Association of Political Science of Uzbekistan	*	*
Venezuelan Political Science Association	1974	*
Yugoslav Political Science Association	1954	*

Total: 35,689 +
*Data not provided.

Source: *Participation* (2000) 24/3: 24–32. Bulletin of the International Political Science Association / Bulletin de l'association internationale de science politique.

Appendix B

INTERNATIONAL POLITICAL SCIENCE ASSOCIATION FIELDS OF INQUIRY— 1997

Main Fields

Central Government
Area Studies
Legislatures
International Relations
Political Executives
International Law
Judicial Systems and Behaviour
Public Administration
Political Parties
Public Policy
Elections and Voting Behaviour
Local and Urban Politics
Pressure Groups
Women and Politics
Political Theory and Philosophy
Developmental Politics
Comparative Politics
Political Science Methods

Research Committees

Conceptual and Terminological Analysis
Political Elites

European Unification
Public Bureaucracies in Developing Societies
Comparative Studies on Local Government and Politics
Political Sociology
Women, Politics, and Developing Nations
Legislative Specialists
Comparative Judicial Studies
Global Policy Studies
Science and Politics
Biology and Politics
Democratization in Comparative Perspective
Politics and Ethnicity
Political Geography
Socio-Political Pluralism
The Emerging International Economic Order
Asian and Pacific Studies
Sex Roles and Politics
Political Finance and Political Corruption
Political Socialization and Education
Political Communication
Political Support and Alienation
Armed Forces and Society
Comparative Health Policy
Human Rights
Structure and Organization of Government
Comperative Federation and Federalism
Psycho-Politics
Comparative Public Opinion
Political Philosophy
Public Policy Analysis
Comparative Study of the Discipline of Political Science
Comparative Representation and Electoral System
Technology and Development
Political Power
Rethinking in Political Development
Politics and Business

Study Groups

The Welfare State and Developing Societies
Public Enterprises and Privatization
New World Orders
Geopolitics
System Integration of Divided Nations
Religion and Politics
Military Rule and Democratization in the Third World
International Data Development
Politics of Global Environmental Change
Local-Global Relations
Administrative Culture
Socialism, Capitalism and Democracy

Source: *Participation* (1997) 21 (3): 53.

Appendix C

AMERICAN POLITICAL SCIENCE ASSOCIATION
FIELDS OF INQUIRY—1998

General Fields (Members on APSA mailing list)

American Government and Politics (4,265)
Comparative Politics (4,340)
International Politics (3,450)
Methodology (1,062)
Political Philosophy and Theory (2,119)
Public Administration (1,240)
Public Law and Courts (1,032)
Public Policy (2,391)

Subfields

Advanced Industrial Societies
Africa
African American Politics
Asian American Politics
Australia
Balkans
Baltics
Bureaucracy and Organizational Behavior
Canada
Caribbean
Central America
Central Asia

China
Civil Rights and Liberties
Conflict Processes
Congress
Constitutional Law and Theory
Criminal Justice
Defense
Developing Nations
East Asia
Economic Policy
Education Policy
Electoral Behavior
Electoral Systems
Energy Policy
Environmental Policy
Ethnic and Racial Politics
Evaluation Research
Executive Politics
Federalism and Intergovernmental Relations
Feminist Theory
Foreign Policy
France
Gender Politics and Policy
Germany
Great Britain
Health Care
History and Politics
Housing
Immigration Policy
India
International Law and Organizations
International Political Economy
International Security
Japan
Judicial Politics

Labor Policy
Latin America
Latino Politics
Leadership Studies
Legislative Studies
Lesbian and Gay Politics
Life Sciences and Politics
Literature and Politics
Mexico
Middle East
Native American Politics
Normative Political Theory
North America
Political Behavior
Political Communication
Political Development
Political Economy
Political Parties and Organizations
Political Psychology
Political Thought: Historical
Positive Political Theory
Post Communist Europe
Post Soviet Region
Presidency
Public Finance and Budgeting
Public Opinion
Regulatory Policy
Religion and Politics
Research Methods
Russia
Scandinavia
Science and Technology
Social Movements
Social Welfare
South Africa

South America
South Asia
Spain
State Politics
Trade
Ukraine
United States
Urban Politics
Western Europe
Women and Politics

Sections (Members on mailing list)

Federalism and Intergovernmental Relations (386)
Law and Courts (757)
Legislative Studies (589)
Public Policy (791)
Political Organizations and Parties (540)
Public Administration (612)
Conflict Processes (281)
Representation and Electoral Systems (326)
Presidency Research (394)
Political Methodology (585)
Religion and Politics (415)
Urban Politics (394)
Science, Technology and Environmental Politics (327)
Women and Politics (560)
Foundations of Political Theory (531)
Computers and Multimedia (238)
International Security and Arms Control (441)
Comparative Politics (1,372)
Politics and Society in Western Europe (390)
State Politics and Policy (362)
Political Communication (381)
Politics and History (585)

Political Economy (612)
Ecological and Transformational Politics (248)
New Political Science (248)
Political Psychology (299)
Undergraduate Education (329)
Politics and Literature (275)
Domestic Sources of Foreign Policy (310)
Elections, Public Opinion and Voting Behavior (632)
Race, Ethnicity and Politics (442)

Source: American Political Science Association, *Mailing Lists to Reach Political Scientists,* 1998.

Appendix D

RELIGIOUS DENOMINATIONS OF CONSCIENTIOUS OBJECTORS IN U.S. WORLD WAR II CIVILIAN PUBLIC SERVICE CAMPS (NUMBER OF MEMBERS IN CPS)

Advent Christian	3
African Methodist Episcopal	1
Ambassadors of Christ	1
Antinsky Church	1
Apostolic	2
Apostolic Christian Church	3
Apostolic Faith Movement	2
Assemblies of God	32
Assembly of Christians	1
Assembly of Jesus Christ	1
Associated Bible Students	36
Baptist, Northern	178
Baptist, Southern	45
Berean Church	1
Bible Students School	1
Body of Christ	1
Brethren Assembly	1
Broadway Tabernacle	1
Buddhist	1
Calvary Gospel Tabernacle	1
Catholic, Roman	149
Christadelphians	127
Christian Brethren	1

Christian Catholic Apostolic	1
Christian Convention	1
Christian Jew	1
Christian & Missionary Alliance	5
Christian Missionary Society	1
Christian Scientist	14
Christ's Church	1
Christ's Church of the Golden Rule	3
Christ's Followers	1
Christ's Sanctified Holy Church	2
Church (The)	1
Church of the Brethren	1,353
Church of Christ	199
Church of Christ Holiness	1
Church of Christian Fellowship	1
Church of England	1
Church of the First Born	11
Church of the Four Leaf Clover	1
Church of the Full Gospel, Inc.	1
Church of God of Abrahamic Faith	13
Church of God of Apostolic Faith	4
Church of God Assembly	1
Church of God in Christ	12
Church of God, Guthrie, Okla.	5
Church of God, Holiness	6
Church of God, Indiana	43
Church of God & Saints of Christ	12
Church of God, Sardis	1
Church of God, Seventh Day	21
Church of God, Tennessee (two bodies)	7
Church of God (several bodies)	33
Church of the Gospel	1
Church of Jesus Christ	1
Church of Jesus Christ, Sullivan, Indiana	15

Church of Light	1
Church of the Living God	2
Church of the Lord Jesus Christ	1
Church of the Open Door	1
Church of the People	1
Church of Radiant Life	1
Church of Truth (New Thought)	1
Circle Mission (Father Divine)	10
Community Churches	12
Congregational Christian	209
Defenders	1
Disciples Assembly of Christians	1
Disciples of Christ	78
Dunkard Brethren	30
Doukhobor (Peace Progressive Society)	3
Elim Covenant Church	1
Emissaries of Divine Light	1
Episcopal	88
Essenes	5
Ethical Culture, Society of	3
Evangelical	50
Evangelical-Congregational	2
Evangelical Mission Convent (Swedish)	11
Evangelical & Reformed	101
Evangelistic Mission	3
Faith Tabernacle	18
Federated Church	1
Filipino Full Gospel	1
Fire Baptized Holiness	3
First Apostolic	1
First Century Gospel	28
First Divine Association in America, Inc.	16
First Missionary Church	2
Followers of Jesus Christ	4

Four Square Gospel	2
Free Holiness	3
Free Methodist	6
Free Pentecostal Church of God	4
Free Will Baptist	2
Friends, Society of (Quakers)	951
Full Gospel Conference of the World, Inc.	4
Full Gospel Mission	3
Full Salvation Union	1
Galilean Mission	1
German Baptist Brethren	157
German Baptist Convention of North America	4
Glory Tabernacle	2
God's Bible School	1
Gospel Century	1
Gospel Chapel	2
Gospel Hall	1
Gospel Meeting Assembly	1
Gospel Mission	2
Gospel Tabernacle	2
Gospel Temple	1
Grace Chapel	1
Grace Truth Assembly	1
Gracelawn Assembly	1
Greek Apostolic	1
Greek Catholic	1
Greek Orthodox	1
Hepzibah Faith	6
Hindu Universal	1
Holiness Baptist	1
Holiness General Assembly	1
House of David	2
House of Prayer	1
Humanist Society of Friends	2

Immanuel Missionary Association	13
Independent Assembly of God	2
Independent Church	2
Institute of Religious Society & Philosophy	1
Interdenominational	16
International Missionary Society	2
Jehovah's Witnesses	409
Jennings Chapel	9
Jewish	60
Kingdom of God	1
Kingdom Missionaries	1
Latin American Council of Christian Churches	1
Lemurian Fellowship	9
Lord our Righteousness	1
Lutheran (nine synods)	108
Lutheran Brethren	2
Mazdaznam	1
Megiddo Mission	1
Mennonites	4,665
Methodist	673
Missionary Church Association	8
Moody Bible Institute	2
Mormons (Church of Jesus Christ of Latter Day Saints	10
Moravian	2
Moslem	1
Multnomah School of the Bible	2
National Baptist Convention, U.S.A., Inc.	5
National Church of Positive Christianity	5
Nazarene, Church of the	23
New Age Church	3
Norwegian Evangelical Free Church	2
Old German Baptist	7
Open Bible Standard	1
Orthodox Parsee Z.	2

Overcoming Faith Tabernacle	1
Oxford Movement	1
Pentecostal Assemblies of Jesus Christ	1
Pentecostal Assemblies of the World	3
Pentecostal Assembly	2
Pentecostal Church, Inc.	2
Pentecostal Evangelical	1
Pentecostal Holiness	6
People's Christian Church	1
People's Church	3
Pilgrim Holiness	3
Pillar of Fire	1
Pillar and Ground of the Truth	1
Placabel Council of Latin Am. Churches	1
Plymouth Brethren	12
Plymouth Christian	1
Presbyterian, U.S	5
Presbyterian, U.S.A.	192
Primitive Advent	2
Progressive Brethren	1
Quakertown Church	1
Reading Road Temple	1
Reformed Church of America (Dutch)	15
Reformed Mission of the Redeemer	1
Rogerine Quakers (Pentecostal Friends)	3
Rosicrusian	1
Russian Molokan (Christian Spiritual Jumpers)	76
Russian Old Testament Church	1
Saint's Mission	1
Salvation Army	1
Sanctified Church of Christ	1
Scandinavian Evangelical	1
Schwenkfelders (Apostolic Christian Church, Inc.	1
School of the Bible	1

Serbian Orthodox	1
Seventh Day Adventist	17
Seventh Day Adventist, Reformed	1
Seventh Day Baptist	3
Shiloh Tabernacle	1
Spanish Church of Jesus Christ	1
Spiritual Mission	1
Spiritualist	1
Swedenborg	1
Taoist	1
Theosophists	14
Trinity Tabernacle	1
Triumph the Church & Kingdom of God in Christ	1
Triumph Church of the New Age	1
True Followers of Christ	1
Truelight Church of Christ	1
Twentieth Century Bible School	5
Unitarians	44
Union Church (Berea, Ky.)	4
Union Mission	1
United Baptist	1
United Brethren	27
United Christian Church	2
United Holiness Church, Inc.	1
United Holy Christian Church of America	2
United International Young People's Assembly	2
United Lodge of Theosophists	2
United Pentecostal Council of the Assemblies of God in America	1
United Presbyterian	12
Unity	3
Universal Brotherhood	1
Universalist	2
War Resister's League	46
Wesleyan Methodist	8

World Student Federation	2
Young Men's Christian Association (YMCA)	2
Zoroastrian	2
Total affiliated with denominations:	10,838
Non-affiliated	449
Denominations unidentified	709
Total:	**11,996**

Source: Anderson 1994: 280-6. Cf. Selective Service System 1950: 318-20

NOTES

Epigraphs: Alfred North Whitehead in Alan L. Mackay, comp., *A Dictionary of Scientific Quotations* (Bristol, UK: Institute of Physics Publishing, 1991), 262. **Chapter 1**: Bertrand Russell, *Wisdom of the West* (New York: Crescent Books, 1977), 10; Jawaharlal Nehru, *An Autobiography* (New Delhi: Oxford University Press, 1982), 409. **Chapter 2**: Daniels and Gilula, 1970: 27. **Chapter 3**: G. Ramachandran, remarks at the Conference on Youth for Peace, University of Kerala, Trivandrum, India, February 23, 1986. **Chapter 4**: Nobel Prize Winners, 1981: 61. **Chapter 5**: Alexis de Tocqueville, quoted in Wilson, 1951: 244; Petra K. Kelly, *Thinking Green!* (Berkeley, Calif.: Parallax Press, 1994), 38. **Chapter 6:** General Douglas MacArthur in Cousins 1987: 69; Martin Luther King, Jr., "The Future of Integration," pamphlet of speech at a Manchester College convocation, North Manchester, Indiana, February 1, 1968, 9; Max Weber in Weber 1958: 128; Gandhi 1958-1994: Vol. XXVI, 1928, 68.

1. Lest this be regarded as too harsh a portrait of patriotic United States lethality, consider the battle cry introduced into the *Congressional Record* on April 16, 1917 by Senator Robert L. Owen, Democrat of Oklahoma, in support of American entry into World War I.

> Mr. President, I found in a western paper a few days ago an editorial in the Muskogee Phoenix, Muskogee Okla., written by Tams Bixby, Esq., former chairman of the Dawes Commission. It breathes a high, pure note of Christian patriotism, which I think deserves a place in our annals at this time. I wish to read it. It is very short. It is entitled:
> ONWARD, CHRISTIAN SOLDIERS!
> The United States of America, given to the world by the Pil-

grim Fathers, through their love and devotion to the Omnipotent ruler of the destinies of men, has declared war on the anniversary of our Savior's crucifixion.

It is altogether fitting and proper that it should be as it is. Loyal Americans will go forth to war not only as the champions of liberty and freedom and humanity but as soldiers of the cross. As He died upon the cross nearly 2,000 years ago for the salvation of mankind Americans will die upon the field of battle to make this a better world.

Through America's blood the world is to be purged of a barbaric, heathenish dynasty that in its lust has forgotten the teachings of our Savior. It is a noble thing to die and to suffer that men may be brought nearer to God.

America, unafraid, girded with the armor of righteousness, strides forth to battle. There is no hatred in our hearts; we bear no malice toward our enemies; we ask no conquest nor material reward. America, true to the traditions that gave her birth, is to wage a noble, Christian war. We are willing to die if need be to bring to all men once more the message of peace on earth, good will. And in this sacred hour America offers for her enemies the prayer of the cross, "Father, forgive them; they know not what they do."

The call to arms has been sounded. America, champion of righteousness, of civilization, and of Christianity, with a clear heart and willing hand, marches forth.
Amid the clamor and the cries of battle come the strains of the hymn of the united allies of mankind: "Onward, Christian Soldier!"

Congressional Record, 65th Cong., 1st sess., 1917, Vol. 55, Pt. 1, 719.

2. The Seville Statement signers were: David Adams, psychology (U.S.A.); S.A. Barnett, ethology (Australia); N.P. Bechtereva, neurophysiology (U.S.S.R.); Bonnie Frank Carter, psychology (U.S.A.); José M. Rodríguez Delgado, neurophysiology (Spain); José Luis Días, ethology (Mexico); Andrzej Eliasz, individual differences psychology (Poland); Santiago Genovés, biological anthropology (Mexico); Benson E. Ginsburg, behavior genetics (U.S.A.); Jo Groebel, social psychology (Federal Republic of Germany); Samir-Kumar Ghosh, sociology (India); Robert Hinde, animal behaviour (U.K.); Richard E. Leakey, physical anthropology (Kenya); Taha H. Malasi, psychiatry (Kuwait); J. Martin Ramírez, psychobiology (Spain); Federico Mayor Zaragoza, biochemistry (Spain); Diana L. Mendoza, ethology (Spain); Ashis Nandy, political psychology (India); John Paul Scott, animal behavior (U.S.A.); and Riitta Wahlström psychology (Finland).
3. The Fellowship Party, 141 Woolacombe Road, Blackheath, London, SE3 8QP, U.K.
4. Bündnis 90/Die Grünen (Alliance 90/The Greens), Bundeshaus, Bonn 53113, Germany.
5. The United States Pacifist Party, 5729 S. Dorchester Avenue, Chicago, Illinois 60617, U.S.A. Internet: http://www.geocities.com/CapitolHill/Lobby/4826.
6. The Sarvodaya Party, Unnithan Farm, Jagatpura, Malaviya Nagar P.O., Jaipur-302017, Rajasthan, India.
7. Transnational Radical Party, 866 UN Plaza, Suite 408, New York, N.Y. 10017, U.S.A. Internet: http://www.agora.stm.it or www.radicalparty.org.
8. The House of Representatives vote was 373 yeas, 50 nays, and 9 not voting. Representatives voting against war: Edward B. Almon, Democrat of Alabama; Mark R. Bacon, Republican of Michigan; Frederick A. Britten, Republican of Illinois; Edward E. Browne, Republican of Wisconsin; John L. Burnett, Democrat of Alabama; William J. Cary, Republican of Wisconsin; Denver S. Church, Democrat of California; John R. Connelly, Democrat of Kansas; Henry A. Cooper, Republican of Wisconsin; James H. Davidson, Republican of Wisconsin; Charles R. Davis, Republician of Minnesota; Perl D. Decker, Democrat of Missouri; Clarence E. Dill, Democrat of Washington; Charles H. Dillon, Republican of South Dakota; Frederick H. Dominick, Democrat of South Carolina; John J. Esch, Republican of Wisconsin; James A. Frear, Republican

of Wisconsin; Charles E. Fuller, Republican of Illinois; Gilbert N. Hauge, Republican of Iowa; Everis A. Hayes, Republican of California; Walter L. Hensley, Democrat of Missouri; Benjamin C. Hilliard, Democrat of Colorado; Harry E. Hull, Republican of Iowa; William L. Igoe, Democrat of Missouri; Royal C. Johnson, Republican of South Dakota; Edward Keating, Democrat of Colorado; Edward J. King, Republican of Illinois; Moses P. Kinkaid, Republican of Nebraska; Claude Kitchin, Democrat of North Carolina; Harold Knutson, Republican of Minnesota; William L. LaFollette, Republican of Washington; Edward E. Little, Republican of Kansas; Meyer London, Socialist of New York; Ernest Lundeen, Republican of Minnesota; Atkins J. McLemore, Democrat of Texas; William E. Mason, Republican of Illinois; Adolphus P. Nelson, Republican of Wisconsin; Charles H. Randall, Prohibitionist of California; Jeannette Rankin, Republican of Montana; Charles F. Reavis, Republican of Nebraska; Edward E. Roberts, Republican of Nevada; William A. Rodenberg, Republican of Illinois; Dorsey W. Shackleford, Democrat of Missouri; Isaac R. Sherwood, Republican of Ohio; Charles H. Sloan, Republican of Nebraska; William H. Stafford, Republican of Wisconsin; Carl C. Van Dyke, Democrat of Minnesota; Edward Voigt, Republican of Wisconsin; Loren E. Wheeler, Republican of Illinois; and Frank P. Woods, Republican of Iowa. *Congressional Record*, 65th Cong., 1st sess., 1917, Vol. 55, Pt. 1, 413.

9. The Senate vote was 82 yeas, 6 nays, and 8 not voting. Senators voting against war: Asle J. Gronna, Republican of North Dakota; Robert M. LaFollette, Republican of Wisconsin; Harry Lane, Democrat of Oregon; George W. Norris, Republican of Nebraska; William J. Stone, Democrat of Missouri; and James K. Vardaman, Democrat of Mississippi. *Congressional Record*, 65th Cong., 1st sess., 1917, Vol. 55, Pt. 1, 261.

10. Nobel prize signers of the Manifesto on the economic "holocaust" were: Vincente Aleixandre (literature, 1977); Hannes Alfven (physics, 1970); Philip Anderson (physics, 1977); Christian Afinsen (chemistry, 1972); Kenneth Arrow (economics, 1972); Julius Axelrod (medicine, 1970); Samuel Beckett (literature, 1969); Baruj Benacerraf (medicine, 1980); Heinrich Böll (literature, 1972); Norman Ernest Borlaug (peace, 1970); Owen Chamberlin (physics, 1959); Mairead Corrigan (peace, 1976); André Cournand (medicine, 1956); Jean Dausset (medicine, 1980); John Carew Eccles (medicine, 1963); Odysseus

Elytis (literature, 1979); Ernst Otto Fischer (chemistry, 1973); Roger Guillemin (medicine, 1977); Odd Hassel (chemistry, 1969); Gerhard Herzberg (chemistry, 1971); Robert Hofstadter (physics, 1961); François Jacob (medicine, 1965); Brian Josephson (physics, 1973); Alfred Kastler (physics, 1966); Lawrence R. Klein (economics, 1980); Polykarp Kusch (physics, 1955); Salvador Luria (medicine, 1969); André Lwoff (medicine, 1965); Seán MacBride (peace, 1974); Cweslaw Milosz (literature, 1980); Eugenio Montale (literature, 1975); Nevill Mott (physics, 1977); Gunnar Myrdal (economics, 1974); Daniel Nathans (medicine, 1978); Philip Noel-Baker (peace, 1959); Adolfo Pérez Esquivel (peace, 1980); Rodney Robert Porter (medicine, 1972); Ilya Prigogine (chemistry, 1977); Isidor Isaac Rabi (physics, 1944); Martin Ryle (physics, 1974); Abdus Salam (physics, 1979); Frederik Sanger (chemistry, 1958 and 1980); Albert Szent-Gyorgyi (medicine, 1937); Hugo Theorell (medicine, 1955); Jan Tinbergen (economics, 1969); Nikolas Tinbergen (medicine, 1973); Charles Hard Townes (physics, 1964); Ulf von Euler (medicine, 1970); George Wald (medicine, 1967); James Dewey Watson (medicine, 1962); Patrick White (literature, 1973); Maurice Wilkins (medicine, 1962); Betty Williams (peace, 1976).

BIBLIOGRAPHY

ABUEVA, JOSE V. 2004. *Towards a Nonkilling Filipino Society: Developing an Agenda for Research, Policy and Action,* Marikina City: Kalayaan College.

ACKERKNECHT, ERWIN H. 1982. *A Short History of Medicine.* Baltimore: Johns Hopkins University Press.

ACKERMAN, Peter and DUVALL, Jack. 2000. *A Force More Powerful: A Century of Nonviolent Conflict.* New York: St. Martin's Press.

_____ and KRUEGLER, C. 1994. *Strategic Nonviolent Conflict.* Westport, Conn.: Praeger.

ADAMS, DAVID *et al.* 1989. Statement on violence. *Journal of Peace Research,* 26: 120–21.

_____ 1997. War is not in our biology: a decade of the Seville statement on violence. In Grisolía et al. 1997: 251–56.

ALMOND, GABRIEL A. 1996. Political science: the history of the discipline. In Goodin and Klingemann 1996: 50–96.

ALPEROVITZ, GAR. 1995. *The Decision to Use the Atomic Bomb.* New York: Alfred A. Knopf.

AMATO, JOSEPH A. 1979. Danilo Dolci: a nonviolent reformer in Sicily. In Bruyn and Rayman 1979: 135–60.

AMNESTY INTERNATIONAL. 2006. *The Death Penalty,* ACT 50/009/2006.

ANDERSON, RICHARD C. 1994. *Peace Was In Their Hearts: Conscientious Objectors in World War II.* Watsonville, Calif.: Correlan Publications.

AQUINO, CORAZON C. 1997. Seeds of nonviolence, harvest of peace: The Philippine revolution of 1986. In Grisolía *et al.* 1997: 227–34.

ARENDT, HANNAH. 1970. *On Violence.* New York: Harcourt, Brace & World.

_____ 1982. *Lectures on Kant's Political Philosophy.* Chicago: University of Chicago Press.

ARISTOTLE. 1962. *The Politics,* trans. T.A. Sinclair. Harmondsworth: Penguin.

ASHE, GEOFFREY. 1969. *Gandhi.* New York: Stein and Day.

AUNG SAN SUU KYI. 1998. *The Voice of Hope.* New York: Seven Stories Press.

BAHÁ'U'LLÁH. 1983. *Gleanings from the Writings of Bahá'u'lláh.* Wilmette, Ill.: Bahá'í Publishing Trust.

BANERJEE, MUKULIKA. 2000. *The Pathan Unarmed*, Karachi & New Delhi: Oxford University Press.

BARBEY, CHRISTOPHE. 2001. *La non-militarisation et les pays sans arm*ée: une réalité! Flendruz, Switzerland: APRED.

BAXTER, ARCHIBALD. 2000. *We Will Not Cease.* Baker, Ore.: The Eddie Tern Press.

BEBBER, CHARLES C. 1994. Increases in U.S. violent crime during the 1980s following four American military actions. *Journal of Interpersonal Violence* 9(1): 109–16.

BEER, MICHAEL. 1994. Annotated bibliography of nonviolent action training. *International Journal of Nonviolence,* 2: 72–99.

BEISNER, ROBERT L. 1968. *Twelve Against Empire: The Anti-Imperialists, 1898–1900.* New York: McGraw-Hill.

BENDAÑA, ALEJANDRO. 1998. "From Guevara to Gandhi." Managua, Nicaragua: Centro de Estudios Internationales.

BENNETT, LERONE JR. 1993. *Before the Mayflower: A History of Black America.* New York: Penguin Books.

BHAVE, VINOBA. 1963. *Shanti Sena,* 2nd ed., trans Marjorie Sykes. Rajghat, Varanasi, India: Sarva Seva Sang Prakashan.

_____ 1994. *Moved by Love: The Memoirs of Vinoba Bhave,* trans. Marjorie Sykes. Hyderabad: Sat Sahitya Sahayogi Sangh.

BING, ANTHONY G. 1990. *Israeli Pacifist: The Life of Joseph Abileah.* Syracuse, N.Y.: Syracuse University Press.

BISWAS, S.C. ed. 1990 (1969). *Gandhi: Theory and Practice.*

Social Impact and Contemporary Relevance. Shimla: Indian Institute of Advanced Study.

BONDURANT, JOAN V. 1969. *Conquest of Violence: The Gandhian Philosophy of Conflict.* Berkeley: University of California Press.

BONTA, BRUCE D. 1993. *Peaceful Peoples: An Annotated Bibliography.* Metuchen, N.J. and London: Scarecrow Press.

_____ 1996. Conflict resolution among peaceful societies: the culture of peacefulness. *Journal of Peace Research,* 33: 403–420.

BOORSTIN, DANIEL J. 1983. *The Discoverers.* New York: Random House.

_____ 1992. *The Creators.* New York: Random House.

_____ 1998. *The Seekers.* New York: Random House.

BOSERUP, ANDERS and MACK, ANDREW. 1974. *War Without Weapons: Non-Violence in National Defence.* New York: Schocken Books.

BOUBALT, GUY; GAUCHARD, BENOÎT; and MULLER, JEAN-MARIE. 1986. *Jacques de Bollardière: Compagnon de toutes les libérations.* Paris: Non-Violence Actualité.

BOULDING, ELISE. 1980. *Women, the Fifth World.* New York: Foreign Policy Association.

_____ 1992. *New Agendas for Peace Research: Conflict and Security Reexamined.* Boulder, Colo.: Lynne Rienner Publishers.

BOURNE, RANDOLPH S. 1964 (1914–1918). *War and the Intellectuals.* New York: Harper & Row.

BROCK, PETER. 1968. *Pacifism in the United States: From the Colonial Era to the First World War.* Princeton: Princeton University Press.

_____ 1970. *Twentieth Century Pacifism.* New York: D. Van Nostrand.

_____ 1972. *Pacifism in Europe to 1914.* Princeton: Princeton University Press.

_____ 1990. *The Quaker Peace Testimony 1660 to 1914.* York, England: Sessions Book Trust.

_____ 1991a. *Studies in Peace History.* York, England: William Sessions Limited.

_____ 1991b. Conscientious objectors in Lenin's Russia: A report, 1924. Pp. 81–93 in *Studies in Peace History.*

_____ 1992. *A Brief History of Pacifism: From Jesus to Tolstoy.* Syracuse, N.Y.: Syracuse University Press.

BROWN, LESTER *et al.* 1997. *State of the World 1997.* New York: W.W. Norton & Company.

_____ GARDNER, GARY; AND HALWEIL, BRIAN. 1999. *Beyond Malthus: Nineteen Dimensions of the Population Challenge.* New York: W.W. Norton.

BRUYN, SEVERYN T. and RAYMAN, PAULA M., eds. 1979. *Nonviolent Action and Social Change.* New York: Irvington Publishers.

BUREAU OF JUSTICE. 2000a. *Capital Punishment 1999.* Washington: U.S. Department of Justice.

_____ 2000b. *Prison and Jail Inmates at Midyear 1999.* Washington, D.C.: U.S. Department of Justice.

BURGESS, JOHN W. 1934. *Reminiscences of an American Scholar.* New York: Columbia University Press.

BURNS, JAMES MACGREGOR. 1978. *Leadership.* New York: Harper & Row.

BURROWES, ROBERT J. 1996. *The Strategy of Nonviolent Defense: A Gandhian Approach.* Albany: State University of New York Press.

BURTON, JOHN. 1979. *Deviance, Terrorism & War: The Process of Solving Unsolved Social and Political Problems.* New York: St. Martin's Press.

_____ 1984. *Global Conflict: The Domestic Sources of International Crisis.* Brighton: Wheatsheaf Books.

_____ 1996. *Conflict Resolution: Its Language and Processes.* Lanham, Md.: Scarecrow Press.

_____ 1997. *Violence Explained: The Sources of Conflict, Violence and Crime and their Prevention.* Manchester: Manchester University Press.

CAMPBELL, DONALD T. and FISKE, DONALD W. 1959. Convergent and discriminant validation by the multitrait-multimethod matrix. *Psychological Bulletin* 56 (2): 81–105.

CANADA, GEOFFREY. 1995. *Fist Stick Knife Gun: A Personal History of Violence in America.* Boston: Beacon Press.

CARNEGIE COMMISSION ON PREVENTING DEADLY CONFLICT. 1997. *Preventing Deadly Conflict: Final Report.* Washington, D.C.: Carnegie Commission on Preventing Deadly Conflict.

CARROLL, BERENICE A. 1998. Looking where the key was lost: feminist theory and nonviolence theory. In Satha-Anand and True 1998: 19–33.

CASE, CLARENCE M. 1923. *Non-Violent Coercion: A Study in Methods of Social Pressure.* London: Allen and Unwin.

CHAPPLE, CHRISTOPHER K. 1993. *Nonviolence to Animals, Earth, and Self in Asian Traditions. Albany: State University of New York Press.*

CHARNY, ISRAEL W. 1982. *How Can We Commit the Unthinkable? Genocide the Human Cancer.* Boulder, Colo.: Westview Press.

CHAUDHURI, ELIANA R. 1998. *Planning with the Poor: The Nonviolent Experiment of Danilo Dolci in Sicily.* New Delhi: Gandhi Peace Foundation.

CHOWDHURY, H.B., ed. 1997. *Asoka 2300.* Calcutta: Bengal Buddhist Association.

CHRISTIAN, R.F. 1978. *Tolstoy's Letters: Volume II 1880-1910.* New York: Charles Scribner's Sons.

CLAUSEWITZ, CARL VON. 1976 (1832). *On War,* ed. and trans. Michael Howard and Peter Paret. Princeton: Princeton University Press.

COMMAGER, HENRY S. 1991. The history of American violence: an interpretation. Pp. 3-28 in *Violence: The Crisis of American Confidence,* ed. Hugh D. Graham. Baltimore: Johns Hopkins Press.

COMMONER, BARRY. 1990. *Making Peace With the Planet.* New York: Pantheon Books.

COMSTOCK, CRAIG. 1971. Avoiding pathologies of defense. Pp. 290–301 in *Sanctions for Evil,* ed. Nevitt Sanford and Craig Comstock. Boston: Beacon Press.

CONSER, WALTER H., Jr.; McCARTHY, RONALD M.; TOSCANO, DAVID J.; and SHARP, GENE., eds. 1986. *Resistance, Politics and the Struggle for Independence.* Boulder, Colo.: Lynne Rienner Publishers.

COOK, PHILIP J. and LUDWIG, JENS. 1997. Guns in America: national survey on private ownership and use of firearms. *Research in Brief,* no. 1026. Washington: National Institute of Justice.

COONEY, ROBERT and MICHALOWSKI, HELEN, eds. 1987. *Power of the People: Active Nonviolence in the United States.* Philadelphia, Penn.: New Society Publishers. (Chief Seattle's message pp. 6–7 has been shown to be a screenwriter's fiction.)

COPPIETERS, BRUNO AND ZVEREV, ALEXEI. 1995. V.C. Bonch-Bruevich and the Doukhobors: on the conscientious-objection policies of the Bolsheviks. *Canadian Ethnic Studies/Etudes Ethniques au Canada* 27(3): 72–90.

COUSINS, NORMAN. 1987. *The Pathology of Power.* New York: W.W. Norton.

CRAIG, LEON H. 1994. *The War Lover: A Study of Plato's Republic.* Toronto: University of Toronto Press.

CROW, RALPH E.; GRANT, PHILIP; and IBRAHIM, SAAD E., eds. 1990. *Arab Nonviolent Political Struggle in the Middle East.* Boulder, Colo.: Lynne Rienner Publishers.

CROZIER, FRANK P. (Brig. Gen.). 1938. *The Men I Killed.* New York: Doubleday.

DALTON, DENNIS. 1993. *Mahatma Gandhi: Nonviolent Power in Action.* New York: Columbia University Press.

DANGE, S.A.; MUKERJEE, H.; SARDESAI, S.G.; and SEN, M. 1977. *The Mahatma: Marxist Evaluation.* New Delhi: People's Publishing House.

DANIELS, DAVID N. and GILULA, MARSHALL F. 1970. Violence and the struggle for existence. In Daniels, Gilula, and Ochberg 1970: 405–43.

_____ GILULA; MARSHALL F.; and OCHBERG, FRANK M., eds. 1970. *Violence and the Struggle for Existence.* Boston: Little, Brown.

DAVIDSON, OSHA G. 1993. *Under Fire: The NRA and the Battle for Gun Control.* New York: Henry Holt.

THE DEFENSE MONITOR. 1972–. Washington, D.C.: Center for Defense Information.

DELLINGER, DAVE. 1970. *Revolutionary Nonviolence.* Indianapolis, Ind.: Bobbs-Merrill.

DENNEN, J.M.G. van der. 1990. Primitive war and the ethnological inventory project. Pp. 247–69 in *Sociobiology and Conflict,* eds. J. van der Dennen and V. Falger. London: Chapman and Hall.

_____ 1995. *The Origin of War.* 2 vols. Groningen: Origin Press.

DENSON, JOHN V., ed. 1997. *The Costs of War: America's Pyrrhic Victories.* New Brunswick, N.J.: Transaction Books.

DHAWAN, GOPINATH. 1957. *The Political Philosophy of Mahatma Gandhi.* Ahmedabad: Navajivan Publishing House.

DISSERTATION ABSTRACTS INTERNATIONAL, 1963–99.

DOGAN, MATTEI and PAHRE, ROBERT. 1990. *Creative Marginality: Innovation at the Intersection of the Social Sciences.* Boulder, Colo.: Westview.

DRAGO, ANTONINO. 1996. When the history of science suggests nonviolence. *The International Journal of Nonviolence* 3: 15–19.

EASWARAN, EKNATH, 1999. *Nonviolent Soldier of Islam.* Tomales, Calif.: Nilgiri Press.

EDGERTON, WILLIAM, ed. 1993. *Memoirs of Peasant Tolstoyans in Soviet Russia.* Bloomington: Indiana University Press.

EIBL-EIBESFELDT, IRENÄUS. 1979. *The Biology of Peace and War: Men, Animals, and Aggression.* New York: Viking Press.

EISENDRATH, MAURICE. 1994. Thou shalt not kill—period. In Polner and Goodman 1994: 139–45.

EISENHOWER, DWIGHT D. 1953. Speech to the American Society of Newspaper Editors, April 16, 1953. Full-page excerpt in *The Wall Street Journal,* May 30, 1985, p. 29.

_____ 1959. BBC TV interview, August 31, 1959. Quoted in Peter Dennis and Adrian Preston, eds., *Soldiers as Statesmen.* New York: Barnes & Noble, 1976, p. 132.

_____ 1961. Farewell broadcast, January 17, 1961. *The Spoken Word,* SW-9403.

EVANS, GWYNFOR. 1973. "Nonviolent Nationalism." New Malden, Surrey: Fellowship of Reconciliation. The Alex Wood Memorial Lecture, 1973.

EVERETT, MELISSA. 1989. *Breaking Ranks.* Philadelphia, Penn.: New Society Publishers.

FABBRO, DAVID. 1978. Peaceful societies: an introduction. *Journal of Peace Research* 15: 67-84.

FEDERAL BUREAU OF INVESTIGATION, U.S. DEPARTMENT OF JUSTICE. 2000. *Crime in the United States 1999.* Washington, D.C.: Federal Bureau of Investigation.

FINER, SAMUEL E. 1997. *The History of Government From the Earliest Times.* New York: Oxford University Press. *Vol. i, Ancient Monarchies and Empires. Vol. ii, The Intermediate Ages. Vol. iii, Empires, Monarchies, and the Modern State.*

FISHER, ROGER and URY, WILLIAM. 1981. *Getting to Yes.* Boston, Mass.: Houghton Mifflin Company.

FOGELMAN, EVA. 1994. *Conscience & Courage: Rescuers of Jews During the Holocaust.* New York: Doubleday.

FOSTER, CATHERINE. 1989. *Women for All Seasons: The Story of the Women's International League for Peace and Freedom.* Athens: University of Georgia Press.

FRANK, JEROME D. 1960. Breaking the thought barrier: psychological challenges of the nuclear age. *Psychiatry* 23: 245–66.

_____ 1993. *Psychotherapy and the Human Predicament,* ed. P.E. Dietz. Northvale, N.J.: Jason Aronson.

FRIEDRICH, CARL J. 1969 (1948). *Inevitable Peace.* New York: Greenwood Press.

FROMM, ERICH. 1973. *The Anatomy of Human Destructiveness.* New York: Holt, Rinehart and Winston.

FRY, A. RUTH. 1986 (1952). *Victories Without Violence.* Santa Fe, N. Mex.: Ocean Tree Books.

FRY, DOUGLAS P. 1994. Maintaining social tranquility: internal and external loci of aggression control. In Sponsel and Gregor 1994: 135–54.

_____ and BJÖRKVIST, KAJ, eds. 1997. *Cultural Variation in Conflict Resolution: Alternatives to Violence.* Mahwah, N.J.: Lawrence Erlbaum Associates, Publishers.

FULLER, JOHN G. 1985. *The Day We Bombed Utah.* New York: Signet Books.

FUNG, YU-LAN. 1952. *History of Chinese Philosophy,* trans. Derke. Bodde. Vol. i. Princeton: Princeton University Press.

FUSSELL, PAUL. 1997. The culture of war. In Denson 1997: 351–8.

GALTUNG, JOHAN. 1969. Violence, peace and peace research. *Journal of Peace Research,* 6: 167–91.

_____ 1984. *There are Alternatives!* Nottingham: Spokesman.

_____ 1990. *The True Worlds: A Transnational Perspective.* New York: The Free Press.

_____ 1992. *The Way is the Goal: Gandhi Today.* Ahmedabad: Gujarat Vidyapith, Peace Research Centre.

_____ 1996. *Peace by Peaceful Means.* London: SAGE Publications.

_____ 1998. *Conflict Transformation by Peaceful Means: TheTranscend Method.* Geneva/Torino: Crisis Environments Training Initiative and Disaster Management Training Programme, United Nations.

GANDHI, MOHANDAS K. 1957(1927–1929). *An Autobiography: The Story of My Experiments with Truth.* Boston, Mass.: Beacon Press.

_____ 1958–1994. *The Collected Works of Mahatma Gandhi.* Vols. 1-100. New Delhi: Publications Division, Ministry of Information and Broadcasting, Government of India.

_____ 1969 (1936–1940). *Towards Non-Violent Politics.* Thanjavur, Tamilnad, India: Sarvodaya Prachuralaya.

_____ 1970. *The Science of Satyagraha,* ed. A.T. Hingorani. Bombay: Bharatiya Vidya Bhavan.

_____ 1971. *The Teaching of the Gita,* ed. A.T. Hingorani. Bombay: Bharatiya Vidya Bhavan.

GARA, LARRY and GARA, LENNA MAE. 1999. *A Few Small Candles: War Resisters of World War II Tell Their Stories.* Kent, Ohio: Kent State University Press.

GARRISON, FIELDING H. 1929. *An Introduction to the History of Medicine.* Philadelphia, Penn.: W.B. Saunders.

GIOGLIO, GERALD R. 1989. *Days of Decision: An Oral History of Conscientious Objectors in the Military in the Vietnam War.* Trenton, N.J.: Broken Rifle Press.

GIORGI, PIERO. 1999. *The Origins of Violence By Cultural Evolution.* Brisbane, Australia: Minerva E&S.

GIOVANNITTI, LEN and FREED, FRED. 1965. *The Decision to Drop the Bomb.* New York: Coward-McCann.

GOLDMAN, RALPH M. 1990. *From Warfare to Party Politics: The Critical Transition to Civilian Control.* Syracuse: Syracuse University Press.

GOODIN, ROBERT E. and KLINGEMANN, HANS-DIETER, eds. 1996. *A New Handbook of Political Science.* Oxford: Oxford University Press.

GREENLEAF, ROBERT K. 1977. *Servant Leadership: An Inquiry into the Nature of Legitimate Power and Greatness.* New York: Paulist Press.

GREGG, RICHARD B. 1966 (1935). *The Power of Nonviolence.* New York: Schocken Books.

GRISOLÍA, JAMES S. et al., eds. 1997. *Violence: From Biology to Society.* Amsterdam: Elsevier.

GROSSMAN, DAVE (Lt. Col.). 1995. *On Killing: The Psychological Cost of Learning to Kill in War and Society.* Boston, Mass.: Little Brown.

_____ and DeGAETANO, GLORIA. 1999. *Stop Teaching Our Kids to Kill.* New York: Crown Publishers.

GUETZKOW, HAROLD. 1955. *Multiple Loyalties: Theoretical Approach to a Problem in International Organization.* Princeton, N.J.: Center for Research on World Political Institutions, Princeton University.

GUSEINOV, A.A., ed. 1993. *Nyenasiliye: Filosofiya, Etika, Politika* (Nonviolence: Philosophy, Ethics, Politics). Moscow: Nauka.

HALBERSTAM, DAVID. 1998. *The Children.* New York: Random House.

HALLIE, PHILIP. 1979. *Lest Innocent Blood Be Shed.* New York: Harper & Row.

HARRIES-JENKINS, GWYN. 1993. Britain: from individual conscience to social movement. In Moskos and Chambers 1993: 67–79.

HAWKLEY, LOUISE. and JUHNKE, JAMES C. 1993. *Nonviolent America: History through the Eyes of Peace.* North Newton, Kans.: Bethel College.

HERMAN, A.L. 1999. *Community, Violence, and Peace.* Albany: State University of New York Press.

HESS, G.D. 1995. An introduction to Lewis Fry Richardson and his mathematical theory of war and peace. *Conflict Management and Peace Science* 14 (1): 77–113.

HOBBES. 1968 (1651). *Leviathan,* ed. C.B. Macpherson. Harmondsworth: Penguin.

HOFSTADTER, RICHARD. 1971. Reflections on violence in the United States. Pp. 3–43 in *American Violence: A Documentary History,* ed. Richard Hofstadter and Michael Wallace. New York: Vintage.

HOLMES, ROBERT L., ed. 1990. *Nonviolence in Theory and Practice.* Belmont, Calif.: Wadsworth.

HORIGAN, DAMIEN P. 1996. On compassion and capital punishment: a Buddhist perspective on the death penalty. *The American Journal of Jurisprudence,* 41: 271–88.

HOREMAN, BART and STOLWIJK, MARC. 1998. *Refusing to Bear Arms: A World Survey of Conscription and Conscientious Objection to Military Service.* London: War Resisters International.

HUSAIN, TARIQ. 1997. "The Leadership Challenges of Human Development." Paper presented at the United Nations University/International Leadership Academy, Amman, Jordan, June 1, 1997.

ISHIDA, TAKESHI. 1974(1968). *Heiwa no seijigaku* (Political Science of Peace), 7th ed. Tokyo: Iwanami Shoten.

IYER, RAGHAVAN N. 1973. *The Political and Moral Thought of Mahatma Gandhi.* New York: Oxford University Press.

JAIN, SAGARMAL, ed.; VARNI, JINENDRA, comp. 1993. *Saman Suttam.* Rajghat, Varanasi: Sarva Seva Sang Prakashan.

JOSEPHSON, HANNAH G. 1974. *Jeannette Rankin: First Lady in Congress.* Indianapolis: Bobbs-Merrill.

JOSEPHSON, HAROLD, ed. 1985. *Biographical Dictionary of Modern Peace Leaders.* Westport, Conn.: Greenwood Press.

KANO, TAKAYOSHI. 1990. The bonobos' peaceable kingdom. *Natural History,* 11: 62–70.

KANT, IMMANUEL. 1939(1795). *Perpetual Peace.* New York: Columbia University Press.

KAPUR, SUDARSHAN. 1992. *Raising Up a Prophet: The African-American Encounter with Gandhi.* Boston, Mass: Beacon Press.

KEELEY, LAWRENCE H. 1996. *War Before Civilizations: The Myth of the Peaceful Savage*. Oxford: Oxford University Press.

KELLY, PETRA K. 1984. *Fighting for Hope.*London: Chatto and Windus.

_____ 1989. Gandhi and the Green Party. *Gandhi Marg,* 11: 192–202.

_____ 1990. "For feminization of power!" Speech to the Congress of the National Organization for Women, San Francisco, June 30, 1990.

_____ 1992. *Nonviolence Speaks to Power.* Honolulu: Center for Nonviolence Planning Project, Matsunaga Institute for Peace, University of Hawai'i. Available at www.globalnonviolence.org.

_____ 1994. *Thinking Green! Essays on Environmentalism, Feminism, and Nonviolence.* Berkeley, Calif.: Parallax Press.

KEYES, GENE. 1982. Force without firepower. *CoEvolution Quarterly,* 34: 4–25.

KEYFITZ, NATHAN. 1966. How many people have lived on earth. *Demography* 3 (2): 581–2.

KHAN, ABDUL K. 1997. "The Khudai Khidmatgar (Servants of God)/Red Shirt Movement in the North-West Frontier Province of British India, 1927–47." Ph.D. diss., History, University of Hawai`i.

KING, MARTIN LUTHER, JR. 1998. *The Autobiography of Martin Luther King,* Jr., ed. Clayborne Carson. New York: Warner Books.

KISHTAINY, KHALID. 1990. Violent and nonviolent struggle in Arab history. In Crow, Grant, and Ibrahim 1990: 41–57.

KOHN, STEPHEN M. 1987. *Jailed for Peace: The History of American Draft Law Violators, 1658-1985.* New York: Praeger.

KONRAD, A. RICHARD. 1974. Violence and the philosopher. *Journal of Value Inquiry,* 8: 37–45.

KOOL, V.K., ed. 1990. *Perspectives on Nonviolence: Recent Research in Psychology.* New York: Springer-Verlag.

_____, ed. 1993. *Nonviolence: Social and Psychological Issues.* Lanham, Md.: University Press of America.

KROPOTKIN, PETER. 1972 (1914). *Mutual Aid: A Factor of Evolution.* New York: New York University Press.

KUHLMANN, JÜRGEN and LIPPERT, EKKEHARD. 1993. The Federal Republic of Germany: conscientious objection as social welfare. In Moskos and Chambers 1993: 98–105.

LAFAYETTE JR., BERNARD and JEHNSEN, DAVID C. 1995. *The Briefing Booklet: An Introduction to The Kingian Nonviolence Reconciliation Program.* Galena, Ohio: Institute for Human Rights and Responsibilities.

_____ 1996. *The Leader's Manual, A Structured Guide and Introduction to Kingian Nonviolence: The Philosophy and*

Methodology. Galena, Ohio: Institute for Human Rights and Responsibilities.

LEWER, NICK and SCHOFIELD, STEVEN, eds. 1997. *Non-Lethal Weapons: A Fatal Attraction!* London: Zed Books.

LEWIS, JOHN. 1973(1940). *The Case Against Pacifism.* Introd. Carl Marzani. New York: Garland.

LIGT, BARTHÉLEMY de. 1972(1938). *The Conquest of Violence: an Essay on War and Revolution,* introds. George Lakey and Aldous Huxley. New York: Garland.

LOCKE, HUBERT G. 1969. *The Detroit Riot of 1967.* Detroit, Mich.: Wayne State University Press.

LOCKE JOHN. 1970 (1689). *Two Treatises of Government,* ed. P. Laskett. Cambridge: Cambridge University Press.

LOPEZ-REYES, RAMON. 1998. The fight/flight response and nonviolence. In Satha-Anand and True 1998: 34–82.

LYND, STAUGHTON and LYND, ALICE, eds. 1995. *Nonviolence in America: A Documentary History.* Maryknoll, N.Y.: Orbis Books.

LYTTLE, BRADFORD. 1982. The apocalypse equation.*Harvard Magazine* (March-April): 19–20.

MACNAIR, RACHEL M. 2002. *Perpetration-Induced Traumatic Stress: The Psychological Consequences of Killing.* Westport, Conn.: Praeger Publishers.

_____ 2003. *The Psychology of Peace: An Introduction.* Westport, Conn.: Praeger Publishers.

MCALLISTER, PAM. 1982. *Reweaving the Web of Life: Feminism and Nonviolence*. Philadelphia, Pa.: New Society Publishers.

_____ 1988. *You Can't Kill the Spirit.* Philadelphia, Pa.: New Society Publishers. Barbara Deming Memorial Series: Stories of Women and Nonviolent Action.

MCCARTHY, COLMAN. 1994. *All of One Peace.* New Brunswick, N.J.: Rutgers University Press.

MCCARTHY, RONALD M. 1997. Methods of nonviolent action. In Vogele and Powers 1997: 319–28. New York: Garland Publishing.

_____ and SHARP, G. 1997. *Nonviolent Action: A Research Guide.* New York and London: Garland Publishing.

MCGUINESS, KATE. 1993. Gene Sharp's theory of power: a feminist critique of consent. *Journal of Peace Research* 30: 101–15.

MCSORLEY, RICHARD. 1985. *New Testament Basis of Peacemaking.* Scottdale, Penn.: Herald Press.

MACGREGOR, G.H.C. 1960. *The Relevance of an Impossible Ideal.* London: Fellowship of Reconciliation.

MACHIAVELLI, NICCOLO. 1961 (1513). *The Prince,* trans. G. Bau. Harmondsworth: Penguin.

MAGUIRE, MAIREAD CORRIGAN. 1999. *The Vision of Peace,* ed. John Dear. Maryknoll, N.Y.: Orbis Books.

MAHAPRAJNA, YUVACHARYA. 1987. *Preksha Dhyana: Theory and Practice.* Ladnun, Rajasthan: Jain Vishva Bharati.

_____ 1994. *Democracy: Social Revolution Through Individual Transformation.* Ladnun, Rajasthan: Jain Vishva Bharati.

MAHONY, LIAM and EGUREN, LUIS E. 1997. *Unarmed Bodyguards.* West Hartford, Conn.: Kumarian Press.

MANN, CORAMAE RICHEY. 1996. *When Women Kill.* Albany: State University of New York Press.

MARTIN, BRIAN. 1989. Gene Sharp's theory of power. *Journal of Peace Research,* 26: 213–22.

_____ et al. 1991. *Nonviolent Struggle and Social Defence.* Ed. S. Anderson and J. Larmore. London: War Resisters International and the Myrtle Solomon Memorial Fund.

_____ 1992. Science for non-violent struggle. *Science and Public Policy,* 19: 55-8.

_____ 2001. *Technology for nonviolent struggle.* London: War Resisters International.

MARX, KARL and ENGELS, FRIEDRICH. 1976(1848). *The Communist Manifesto,* introd. A.J.P. Taylor. Harmondsworth: Penguin.

MAYOR, FEDERICO. 1995. *The New Page.* Paris: UNESCO Publishing.

MERCY, JAMES A. and SALTZMAN, LINDA E. 1989. Fatal violence among spouses in the United States 1976–85. *American Journal of Public Health* 79 (5): 595–9.

MOGIL, CHRISTOPHER; and SLEPIAN, ANN; with WOODROW, PETER. 1993. *We Gave a Fortune Away.* Gabriola Island, B.C.: New Society Publishers.

MORGAN, ROBIN, ed. 1984. *Sisterhood is Global.* Garden City, N.Y.: Anchor Press/Doubleday.

MORRISEY, WILL. 1996. *A Political Approach to Pacifism.* 2 vols. Lewiston, N.Y.: Edwin Mellen Press.

MORTON, BRUCE E. 2000. "The Dual Quadbrain Model of Behavioral Laterality." Department of Biochemistry and Biophysics, School of Medicine, University of Hawai'i.

MOSER-PUANGSUWAN, YESHUA and WEBER, THOMAS. 2000. *Nonviolent Intervention Across Borders: A Recurrent Vision.*Honolulu: Spark M.Matsunaga Institute for Peace, University of Hawai'i.

MOSKOS, CHARLES and CHAMBERS, JOHN W. II, eds. 1993. *The New Conscientious Objectors: From Sacred to Secular Resistance.* Oxford: Oxford University Press.

NAGLER, MICHAEL N. 1982. *America Without Violence.* Covelo, Calif.: Island Press.

_____ 2001. *Is There No Other Way? The Search for a Nonviolent Future.* Berkeley, Calif.: Berkeley Hills Books.

NAHAL, CHAMAN. 1997. A sister remembered. *The Hindustan Times,* New Delhi, November 10.

NAKAMURA, HAJIME. 1967. Basic features of legal, economic, and political thought in Japan. Pp. 143–63 in *The Japanese Mind,* ed. Charles A. Moore. Honolulu: East-West Center and University of Hawaii Press.

NARAYAN, JAYAPRAKASH. 1975. From socialism to sarvodaya. Pp. 145–77 in *Jayaprakash Narayan,* Ajit Bhattacharya. Delhi: Vikas.

_____ 1978. *Towards Total Revolution.* 4 vols., ed. Brahmanand. Bombay: Popular Prakashan.

NATHAN, OTTO and NORDEN, HEINZ, eds. 1968. *Einstein on Peace.* New York: Schocken Books.

NAUTIYAL, ANNPURNA. 1996. Chipko movement and the women of Garhwal Himalaya. *Gandhian Perspectives* 9 (2): 9–17.

NOBEL PRIZE RECIPIENTS. 1981. Manifesto of Nobel prize winners. *IFDA Dossier,* 25: 61–63.

NORMAN, LIANE E. 1989. *Hammer of Justice: Molly Rush and the Plowshares Eight.* Pittsburgh, Pa.: Pittsburgh Peace Institute.

ORGANIZATION OF AMERICAN HISTORIANS. 1994. Peacemaking in American history. *Magazine of History,* 8(3): 1–96.

PAIGE, GLENN D. 1968. *The Korean Decision: June 24-30, 1950.* New York: Free Press.

_____ 1971. Some implications for political science of the comparative politics of Korea. Pp. 139–68 in *Frontiers of Development Administration,* ed. Fred W. Riggs. Durham, N.C.: Duke University Press.

_____ 1977. *The Scientific Study of Political Leadership.* New York: Free Press.

_____ 1977. On values and science: *The Korean Decision* reconsidered. *American Political Science Review* 71(4): 1603–9.

_____ 1986. Beyond the limits of violence: toward nonviolent global citizenship. Pp. 281-305 in *Textbook on World Citizenship,* ed. Young Seek Choue. Seoul: Kyung Hee University Press.

_____ and GILLIATT, SARAH, eds. 1991. *Buddhism and Nonviolent Global Problem-Solving: Ulan Bator Explorations.* Honolulu: Center for Global Nonviolence Planning Project, Matsunaga Institute for Peace, University of Hawai'i. Available at www.globalnonviolence.org.

_____; SATHA-ANAND, CHAIWAT; AND GILLIATT, SARAH, eds. 1993a. *Islam and Nonviolence.* Honolulu: Center for Global Nonviolence Planning Project, Matsunaga

Institute for Peace, University of Hawai'i. Available at www.globalnonviolence.org.

_____ 1993b. *To Nonviolent Political Science: From Seasons of Violence.* Honolulu: Center for Global Nonviolence Planning Project, Matsunaga Institute for Peace, University of Hawai'i. Available at www.globalnonviolence.org.

_____ and ROBINSON, JAMES A. 1998. In memoriam: Richard Carlton Snyder. *PS: Political Science & Politics,* 31: 241–2.

_____ 1999. Gandhi as leader: a Plutarchan perspective. *Biography: An Interdisciplinary Quarterly* 22 (1): 57–74.

_____ 1999. A question for the systems sciences: is a nonkilling society possible? Pp. 409–16 in Yong Pil Rhee, ed. *Toward New Paradigm of Systems Sciences.* Seoul: Seoul National University Press.

PALMER, STUART H. 1960. *A Study of Murder.* New York: Thomas Y. Crowell.

PAREKH, BHIKHU. 1989a. *Colonialism, Tradition and Reform: An Analysis of Gandhi's Political Discourse.* Newbury Park: Sage.

_____ 1989b. *Gandhi's Political Philosophy: A Critical Examination.* London: Macmillan.

PARKIN, SARA. 1994. *The Life and Death of Petra Kelly.* London: Pandora, HarperCollins Publishers.

PBS. 1993. "Fame in the 20th Century." Part V.

PEACE NEWS. 1998. Las Abejas: the Bees continue to fly. July: 12–14.

PELTON, LEROY H. 1974. *The Psychology of Nonviolence.* New York: Pergamon Press.

PERRIN, NOEL. 1979. *Giving up the Gun.* Boston: David R. Godine Publisher.

PLATO. 1974. *The Republic,* trans. D. Lee. Harmondsworth: Penguin.

PLIMAK, E.G. and KARYAKIN, YU.F. 1979. "Lenin o mirnoi i nyemirnoi formakh revolyutsionnogo perekhoda v sotsializmu" (Lenin on peaceful and nonpeaceful forms of revolutionary transition to socialism). Paper presented to the XIth World Congress of the International Political Science Association, Moscow University, 12–18 August.

PLUTARCH. 1967–75. *Plutarch's Lives.* 11 vols. Trans. B. Perrin. Cambridge, Mass.: Harvard University Press.

POLNER, MURRAY and GOODMAN, NAOMI, eds. 1994. *The Challenge of Shalom.* Philadelphia, Penn.: New Society Publishers.

_____ and O'GRADY, J. 1997. *Disarmed and Dangerous: The Radical Lives and Times of Daniel and Philip Berrigan.* New York: Basic Books.

POWERS, ROGER S. and VOGELE, WILLIAM B., eds. 1997. *Protest, Power and Change: An Encyclopedia of Nonviolent Action from ACT-UP to Women's Suffrage.* New York & London: Garland Publishing.

RADHAKRISHNAN, N. 1992. *Gandhi, Youth & Nonviolence: Experiments in Conflict Resolution.* Mithrapuram, Paranthal Post, Kerala, India: Centre for Development & Peace.

_____. 1997a. *Gandhian Nonviolence: A Trainer's Manual.* New Delhi: Gandhi Smriti and Darshan Samiti.

_____ 1997b. *The Message of Gandhi through Universities.* New Delhi: Gandhi Smriti and Darshan Samiti.

RAMACHANDRAN, G. 1984. *Adventuring With Life: An Autobiography.* Trivandrum, India: S.B. Press.

_____ and MAHADEVAN, T.K., eds. 1970. *Quest for Gandhi.* New Delhi: Gandhi Peace Foundation.

RAMSEY, L. THOMAS. 1999. "How many people have ever lived, Keyfitz's calculation updated." http://www.math.hawaii.edu/`ramsey/People.html.

RANDLE, MICHAEL. 1993. *Civil Resistance.* London: Fontana Press.

RESTAK, RICHARD M. 1979. *The Brain: The Last Frontier.* Garden City, N.Y.: Doubleday.

ROBARCHEK, CLAYTON and ROBARCHEK, CAROLE. 1998. *Waorani: The Contexts of Violence and War.* Fort Worth, Tex.: Harcourt Brace College Publishers.

ROBERTS, ADAM. 1967. *The Strategy of Civilian Defense: Non-Violent Resistance to Aggression.* London: Faber & Faber.

_____ 1975. Civilian resistance to military coups. *Journal of Peace Research,* 12(1): 19–36.

ROLLAND, ROMAIN. 1911. *Tolstoy,* trans. Bernard Miall. New York: E.P. Dutton.

ROODKOWSKY, MARY. 1979. Feminism, peace, and power. In Bruyn and Rayman 1979: 244–66.

ROSENBERG, MARK L. and MERCY, JAMES A. 1986. Homicide: epidemiologic analysis at the national level. *Bulletin of the New York Academy of Medicine,* 62: 376–99.

ROUSSEAU, JEAN-JACQUES. 1966 (1762). *Du contrat social,* introd. Pierre Burgelin. Paris: Garnier-Flammarion.

_____ 1994 (1762). *The Social Contract,* trans. C. Betts. Oxford: Oxford University Press.

ROUSSELL, VINCENT. *Jacques de Bollardière: De l'armée à la non-violence.* Paris: Desclée de Brouwer.

ROYAL SWEDISH ACADEMY OF SCIENCES. 1983. *Ambio* 12. Special issue on environmental research and management priorities for the 1980s.

ROYCE, JOSEPH. 1980. Play in violent and non-violent cultures. *Anthropos,* 75: 799–822.

RUMMEL, RUDOLPH J. 1994. *Death by Governments.* New Brunswick, N.J.: Transaction Publishers.

SAGAN, ELI. 1979. *The Lust to Annihilate: A Psychoanalytic Study of Violence in Greek Culture.* New York: Psychohistory Press.

SALLA, MICHAEL E. 1992. "Third Party Intervention in Interstate Conflict: The International Implications of Groups Committed to Principled Nonviolence in the Thought of M.K. Gandhi, Martin Luther King, Helder Camara & Danilo Dolci." Ph.D. diss., Government, University of Queensland.

SANTIAGO, ANGELA S. 1995. *Chronology of a Revolution 1986.* Manila: Foundation for Worldwide People Power.

SATHA-ANAND, CHAIWAT. 1981. "The Nonviolent Prince." Ph.D. diss., Political Science, University of Hawai'i.

_____ (Qader Muheideen). 1990. The nonviolent crescent: eight theses on Muslim nonviolent action. In Crow, Grant, and Ibrahim 1990: 25–40.

_____ and TRUE, MICHAEL, eds. 1998. *The Frontiers of Nonviolence.* Bangkok and Honolulu: Peace Information Center and Center for Global Nonviolence. In cooperation with the Nonviolence Commission, International Peace Research Association (IPRA).

_____ 1999. Teaching nonviolence to the states. Pp. 186-95 in *Asian Peace: Regional Security and Governance in the Asia-Pacific,* ed. Majid Tehranian. London: I.B. Taurus Publishers.

SCHLISSEL, LOUISE. 1968. *Conscience in America: A Documentary History of Conscientious Objection in America 1757–1967.* New York: E.P. Dutton.

SCHMID, ALEX P. 1985. *Social Defence and Soviet Military Power: An Inquiry Into the Relevance of an Alternative Defence Concept.* Leiden: Center for the Study of Social Conflict, State University of Leiden.

SCHWARTZ, STEPHEN I., ed. 1998. *Atomic Audit: The Costs and Consequences of U.S. Nuclear Weapons Since 1940.* Washington, D.C.: Brookings Institution Press.

SCHWARZSCHILD, STEVEN et al., n.d. *Roots of Jewish Nonviolence.* Nyack, N.Y.: Jewish Peace Fellowship.

SEBEK, VIKTOR. 1983. Bridging the gap between environmental science and policy-making: why public policy often fails to reflect current scientific knowledge. *Ambio,* 12: 118–20.

SELECTIVE SERVICE SYSTEM. 1950. *Conscientious Objection.* Special monograph. No. 11, Vol. i.

SEMELIN, JACQUES. 1994. *Unarmed Against Hitler: Civilian Resistance in Europe, 1939–1943.* Westport, Conn.: Praeger.

SETHI, V.K. 1984. *Kabir: The Weaver of God's Name.* Punjab, India: Radha Soami Satsang Beas.

SHARP, GENE. 1960. *Gandhi Wields the Weapon of Moral Power.* Ahmedabad: Navajivan Publishing House.

_____ 1973. *The Politics of Nonviolent Action.* Boston, Mass.: Porter Sargent.

_____ 1979. *Gandhi As a Political Strategist*. Boston, Mass.: Porter Sargent.

_____ 1980. *Social Power and Individual Freedom*. Boston, Mass.: Porter Sargent.

_____ 1989. "The Historical Significance of the Growth of Nonviolent Struggle in the Late Twentieth Century." Paper presented at the Institute of World History of the Academy of Sciences of the USSR, Moscow, November 21–23.

_____ 1990. *Civilian-Based Defense: A Post-Military Weapons System*. Princeton, N.J.: Princeton University Press.

_____ 1993. *From Dictatorship to Democracy*. Cambridge, Mass.: The Albert Einstein Institution.

_____ 1994. "Nonviolent Struggle: A Means toward Justice, Freedom and Peace." A presentation during the mass on Public Education Day, January 18, 1994, sponsored by the Justice and Peace Commission of the Union of Superiors General of the Catholic Church, Rome.

SHRIDHARANI, KRISHNALAL. 1962(1939). *War without Violence*. Bombay: Bharatiya Vidya Bhavan.

SHUB, DAVID. 1976. *Lenin*. Harmondsworth: Penguin Books.

SIBLEY, MULFORD Q., ed. 1963. *The Quiet Battle: Writings on the Theory and Practice of Non-violent Resistance*. Boston, Mass.: Beacon Press.

SIMON, DAVID. 1991. *Homicide: A Year on the Killing Streets*. Boston, Mass.: Houghton Mifflin.

SIVARD, RUTH LEGER. 1996. *World Military and Social Expenditures 1996*. Washington, D.C.: World Priorities. 16th edition.

SNYDER, RICHARD C.; BRUCK, HENRY W.; and SAPIN, BURTON, eds. 1962. *Foreign Policy Decision-Making: An Approach to the Study of International Politics*. New York: The Free Press of Glencoe, Macmillan.

_____ and WILSON, H.H. 1949. *Roots of Political Behavior*. New York: American Book Company.

SOLOMON, GEORGE F. 1970. Psychodynamic aspects of aggression, hostility, and violence. In Daniels, Gilula, and Ochberg 1970: 53–78.

SOROKIN, PITIRIM A. 1948. *The Reconstruction of Humanity.* Boston: Beacon Press.

_____ 1954. *The Ways and Power of Love.* Boston: Beacon Press.

SOROS, GEORGE. 1997. The capitalist threat. *The Atlantic Monthly,* February: 45–58.

SPONSEL, LESLIE E. 1994a. The mutual relevance of anthropology and peace studies. In Sponsel and Gregor 1997: 11–19.

_____ and GREGOR, THOMAS, eds. 1994b. *The Anthropology of Peace and Nonviolence.* Boulder, Colo.: Lynne Rienner.

_____ 1996. Peace and nonviolence. Pp. 908–12 in *The Encyclopedia of Cultural Anthropology,* eds. David Levinson and Melvin Ember. New York: Henry Holt.

STANFIELD, JOHN H., II. 1993. The dilemma of conscientious objection for African Americans. In Moskos and Chambers 1993: 47–56.

STANNARD, DAVID E. 1992. *American Holocaust: Columbus and the Conquest of the New World.* Oxford: Oxford University Press.

STEGER, MANFRED B. 2000. *Gandhi's Dilemma.* New York: St. Martin's Press.

_____ and LIND, NANCY S, eds. 1999. *Violence and Its Alternatives.* New York: St. Martin's Press.

STEIN, MICHAEL B. 1997. Recent approaches to the concept of creativity and innovation in political and social science: a summary assessment. Paper presented to the XVIIth World Congress of the International Political Science Association, Seoul, Korea.

STEINSON, BARBARA J. 1980. "The mother half of humanity": American women in the peace and preparedness movements of World War I. Pp. 259–284 in *Women, War, and Revolution,* eds. Carol R. Berkin and Clara M. Lovett. New York and London: Holmes & Meier.

STEPHENSON, CAROLYN M. 1997. Greenpeace. In Vogele and Powers 1997: 220–2.

STEVENS, JOHN. 1987. *Abundant Peace: The Biography of Morihei Ueshiba Founder of Aikido.* Boston: Shambala.

STONE, I.F. 1989. *The Trial of Socrates.* New York: Anchor Books.

SUMMY, RALPH. 1988. Towards a nonviolent political science. Pp. 161-172 in *Professions in the Nuclear Age,* eds. S. Sewell, A. Kelly and L. Daws. Brisbane: Boolarong Publications.

_____ 1991. Vision of a nonviolent society: what should be society's aims. *Balance,* 3(4): 3–8.

_____ 1994. Nonviolence and the case of the extremely ruthless opponent. *Pacifica Review,* 6(1): 1–29.

_____ and SAUNDERS, MALCOLM. 1995. Why peace history? *Peace & Change* 20: 7–38.

_____ 1997. Australia, a history of nonviolent action. In Powers and Vogele 1997: 25–32.

_____ 1998. Nonviolent speech. *Peace Review* 10 (4): 573–8.

SUTHERLAND, BILL and MEYER, MATT. 2000. *Guns and Gandhi in Africa.* Trenton, N.J. and Asmara, Eritrea: Africa World Press.

TARASOFF, KOOZMA J. 1995. Doukhobor survival through the centuries. *Canadian Ethnic Studies/Etudes Ethniques au Canada* 27(3): 4–23. Special Issue: From Russia with Love: The Doukhobors.

TAYYEBULLA, M. 1959. *Islam and Non-Violence.* Allahabad: Kitabistan.

TENDULKAR, D.G. 1967. *Abdul Ghaffar Khan: Faith is a Battle.* Bombay: Popular Prakashan.

THOMPSON, HENRY O. 1988. *World Religions in War and Peace.* Jefferson, N.C. and London: McFarland & Company.

TOBIAS, MICHAEL. 1991. *Life Force: The World of Jainism.* Berkeley, Calif.: Asian Humanities Press.

TOLSTOY, LEO. 1974(1893 and 1894-1909). *The Kingdom of God and Peace Essays,* trans. Aylmer Maude. London: Oxford University Press.

TROCMÉ, ANDRÉ. 1974. *Jesus and the Nonviolent Revolution.* Scottdale, Penn.: Herald Press.

TRUE, MICHAEL. 1995. *An Energy Field More Intense Than War: The Nonviolent Tradition and American Literature.* Syracuse, N.Y.: Syracuse University Press.

TSAI, LOH SENG. 1963. Peace and cooperation among natural enemies: educating a rat-killing cat to cooperate with a hooded rat. *Acta Psychologia Taiwanica,* 3: 1–5.

TWAIN, MARK. 1970(1923). *The War Prayer.* New York: Harper & Row.

UNITED NATIONS. 1978. Final Document of Assembly Session on Disarmament 23 May–1 July 1978. S-10/2. New York: Office of Public Information.

_____ 1993. *Agenda 21: The United Nations Programme of Action from Rio.* New York: United Nations.

_____ 1996. Report of the Fourth World Conference on Women, Beijing, 4 –15 September 1995. New York: United Nations.

UNNITHAN, N. PRABHA; HUFF-CORZINE, LIN; CORZINE, JAY; and WHITT, HUGH P. 1994. *The Currents of Lethal Violence: An Integrated Model of Suicide and Homicide.* Albany: State University of New York Press.

UNNITHAN, T.K.N. and SINGH, YOGENDRA. 1969. *Sociology of Non-Violence and Peace.* New Delhi: Research Council for Cultural Studies, India International Centre.

_____ 1973. *Traditions of Nonviolence.* New Delhi: Arnold-Heinemann India.

UNREPRESENTED NATIONS AND PEOPLES ORGANIZATION (UNPO). 1998a. *Nonviolence and Conflict: Conditions for Effective Peaceful Change.* The Hague: Office of the Secretary General, UNPO. http://www.unpo.org.

_____ 1998b. *Yearbook 1997,* ed. J. Atticus Ryan. The Hague: Kluwer Law International.

VILLAVINCENCIO-PAUROM, RUBY. 1995. Nature/gunless society: utopia within reach. Pp. 146–51 in Emelina S. Almario and Asuncion D. Maramba, eds. *Alay sa Kalinaw:*

Filipino Leaders for Peace. Makati City: Aurora Aragon Quezon Peace Foundation and UNESCO National Commission of the Philippines.

WAAL, FRANS de. 1989. *Peacemaking Among Primates.* Cambridge, Mass.: Harvard University Press.

_____ 1996. *Good Natured: The Origins of Right and Wrong in Humans and Other Animals.* Cambridge, Mass.: Harvard University Press.

_____ 1997. *Bonobo: The Forgotten Ape.* Berkeley: University of California Press.

WALKER, CHARLES C. 1979. Nonviolence in Africa. In Bruyn and Rayman 1979: 186–212.

WAR RESISTERS LEAGUE. 1989. *Handbook for Nonviolent Action.* New York: War Resisters League.

WASHINGTON, JAMES M., ed. 1986. *A Testament of Hope: the Essential Writings and Speeches of Martin Luther King,* Jr. New York: HarperCollins Publishers.

WASSERMAN, HARVEY. 1982. *Killing Our Own: The Disaster of America's Experience With Atomic Radiation.* New York: Delacorte Press.

WATSON, PETER. 1978. *War on the Mind: The Military Uses and Abuses of Psychology.* New York: Basic Books.

WEBER, MAX. 1958(1919). Politics as a vocation. Pp. 77–128 in *From Max Weber: Essays in Sociology,* ed. H.H. Gerth and C. Wright Mills. New York: Oxford University Press.

WEBER, THOMAS. 1989. *Hugging the Trees: The Story of the Chipko Movement.* New Delhi: Penguin.

_____ 1996. *Gandhi's Peace Army: The Shanti Sena and Unarmed Peacekeeping.* Syracuse, N.Y.: Syracuse University Press.

_____ 1997. *On the Salt March: The Historiography of Gandhi's March to Dandi.* New Delhi: HarperCollins Publishers India.

WEEKS, JOHN R. 1996. *Population.* 6th edition. Belmont, Calif.: Wadsworth Publishing.

WEINBERG, ARTHUR and WEINBERG, LILA. 1963. *Instead of Violence: Writings of the Great Advocates of Peace and Nonviolence throughout History.* Boston, Mass.: Beacon Press.

WHIPPLE, CHARLES K. 1839. *Evils of the Revolutionary War.* Boston, Mass.: New England Non-Resistance Society.

_____ 1860a. *Non-Resistance Applied to the Internal Defense of a Community.* Boston, Mass.: R.F. Wallcut.

_____ 1860b. *The Non-Resistance Principle: With Particular Attention to the Help of Slaves by Abolitionists.* Boston, Mass.: R.F. Wallcut.

WHITMAN, WALT. 1855. "Song of myself," *Leaves of Grass,* 42: 33-42. Norwalk, Conn.: The Easton Press.

WILCOCK, EVELYN. 1994. *Pacifism and the Jews.* Landsdown, Gloucestershire: Hawthorn Press.

WILSON, H. HUBERT. 1951. *Congress: Corruption and Compromise.* New York: Rinehart.

WITTNER, LAWRENCE S. 1993. *One World or None: A History of the World Nuclear Disarmament Movement Through 1953.* Stanford, Calif.: Stanford University Press.

_____ 1997. *Resisting the Bomb: A History of the World Nuclear Disarmament Movement, 1954-1970.* Stanford, Calif.: Stanford University Press.

WORLD BANK. 1997. *World Development Report 1997: The State in a Changing World.* Oxford: Oxford University Press.

_____ 1999. Press briefing, "Poverty Update." Washington, D.C., June 2.

WORLD HEALTH ORGANIZATION. 2002. *World Report on Violence and Health.* Geneva: World Health Organization.

WORLD WILDLIFE FUND. 1986. *The Assisi Declarations: Messages on Man and Nature From Buddhism, Christianity, Hinduism, Jainism & Judaism.* Gland, Switzerland: WWF International.

WRANGHAM, RICHARD and PETERSON, DALE. 1996. *Demonic Males: Apes and Origins of Human Violence.* New York: Houghton Mifflin.

YODER, JOHN H. 1983. *What Would You Do? A Serious Answer to a Standard Question.* Scottdale, Penn.: Herald Press.

YOUNG, ANDREW. 1996. *An Easy Burden: The Civil Rights Movement and the Transformation of America.* New York: HarperCollins Publishers.

YOUNG, ART. 1975. *Shelley and Nonviolence.* The Hague: Mouton.

YOUTH DIVISION OF SOKA GAKKAI. 1978. *Cries for Peace: Experiences of Japanese Victims of World War II.* Tokyo: The Japan Times.

ZAHN, GORDON. 1964. In *Solitary Witness: The Life and Death of Franz Jägerstätter.* New York: Holt, Rinehart and Winston.

ZAVERI, ZETHA LAL S. and KUMAR, MAHENDRA. 1992. *Neuroscience & Karma: The Jain Doctrine of Psycho-Physical Force.* Ladnun, Rajasthan: Jain Vishva Bharati.

ZHANG, YI-PING. 1981. Dui feibaoli zhuyi ying jiben kending (We should positively affirm nonviolence). *Shijie lishi* (World History), 16(3): 78–80.

ZIMRING, FRANKLIN E. and HAWKINS, GORDON E. 1986. *Capital Punishment and the American Agenda.* Cambridge: Cambridge University Press.

ZINN, HOWARD. 1980. *A People's History of the United States.* New York: Harper & Row.

ZUNES, STEPHEN; KURTZ, LESTER R.; and ASHER, SARAH BETH, eds. 1999. *Nonviolent Social Movements: A Geographical Perspective.* Oxford: Blackwell Publishers.

INDEX OF NAMES

A

B

C

D

E

F

G

H

I

J

K

L

M

N

O

P

R

S

T

U

V

W

Y

Z

INDEX OF SUBJECTS

A

B

C

D

E

F

G

H

I

J

K

L

M

N

P

Q

R

S

T

U

V

W